PHARMACY FOR THE SOUL

ALSO BY OSHO

Your Answers Questioned
Autobiography of a Spiritually Incorrect Mystic
The Book of Secrets
India My Love: A Spiritual Journey
Love, Freedom, and Aloneness
Meditation: The First and Last Freedom
Sex Matters
Art of Tea
Osho Transformation Tarot
Osho Zen Tarot
Tarot in the Spirit of Zen
Tao: The Pathless Path
Zen: The Path of Paradox
Yoga: The Science of the Soul

INSIGHTS FOR A NEW WAY OF LIVING SERIES

Awareness: The Key to Living in Balance
Courage: The Joy of Living Dangerously
Creativity: Unleashing the Forces Within
Intimacy: Trusting Oneself and the Other
Intuition: Knowing Beyond Logic
Joy: The Happiness That Comes from Within
Maturity: The Responsibility of Being Oneself

AUDIO

Book of Secrets: Keys to Love and Meditation
Osho Meditations on Buddhism
Osho Meditations on Sufism
Osho Meditations on Tantra
Osho Meditations on Tao
Osho Meditations on Yoga
Osho Meditations on Zen

PHARMACY
FOR THE
SOUL

A Comprehensive Collection of
Meditations, Relaxation and Awareness
Exercises, and Other Practices for Physical
and Emotional Well-Being

OSHO

ST. MARTIN'S GRIFFIN

NEW YORK

www.stmartins.com

Created from selected excerpts from the archive of original works by the author
Compiled by Maneesha James
Edited by Sarito Carol Neiman

Book design by Ellen Cipriano

Library of Congress Cataloging-in-Publication Data

Osho, 1931–1990.
    Pharmacy for the soul : a comprehensive collection of meditations, relaxation and awakeness exercises, and other practices for physical and emotional well-being / Osho.
        p. cm.
    ISBN 0-312-32076-0
    EAN 978-0312-32076-8
    1. Conduct of life. 2. Health. 3. Self-help techniques. I. Title.
    BJ1581.2.O75 2004
    299'.93—dc22

                                                                        2003019124

10 9 8 7 6 5 4 3

NOTE TO READER

Any advice or teachings given in this book are not intended to replace the services of your physician, psychotherapist, or psychiatrist. Nor is the book meant to provide an alternative to professional medical treatment. This book offers no medical diagnosis of or treatment for any specific medical or psychological problems you may have. Some of the meditations include strenuous physical activity—if you have any reason to be concerned about the effects of such activity on your health, you should consult your physician before trying these meditations.

CONTENTS

FOREWORD

The relationship of stress to a variety of physical illnesses is by now well known. In the United States, it is estimated that stress helps to account for two-thirds of family doctor visits, and according to the U.S. Center for Disease Control and Prevention, it is a significant contributor to half the deaths in Americans under the age of 65. It has been predicted that by 2020, five of the top ten medical problems worldwide will be stress related.

But in today's environment, it's often difficult for people to balance the overwhelming demands of work, family, and community with the need to take time out for rest and relaxation. All too often our approach to dealing with stress comes down to having a drink or two in the evening, or taking the occasional over-the-counter sleeping pill.

Pharmacy for the Soul offers a wide variety of simple, non-chemical techniques for dealing with the symptoms of stress. In its pages you'll find remedies for everything from tension headaches to insomnia, from the vague feelings of discomfort we all experience at one time or another to very specific issues such as trying to quit smoking or changing your relationship to what and how much you eat.

Because bringing our lives into a more harmonious balance between work and play, stress and relaxation, responsibilities and freedoms isn't just about finding ways to combat stress—it's also about discovering and nourishing the inner wisdom of the spirit that knows what we need and will tell us how to get it if we just take the time to listen. This understanding runs like a thread through the pages of *Pharmacy for the Soul*, and the organization of the book is based on it. Each of us is uniquely individual and responsible for our own lives—*and* each of us is involved with unique and individual others in a dance that can sometimes have us stepping on one another's toes and causing upsets. Learning both how to love better and how to fight better, when it's needed, is all part of bringing more balance, centering, and harmony to our lives.

The techniques offered in the book have been selected with the understanding that many of us simply don't have the time or the opportunity to set aside an hour or more a day for meditation. So there is an abundance of things you can do for a few minutes before you go to bed, or as you wake up in the morning. There are techniques for which it's obvious that you will want privacy, and there are also plenty of things you can do at your desk, on a public bus, or during a walk through the park and nobody will have a clue what you're up to. There are even things you can do with your partner that can bring a different kind of intimacy to your relating.

Finally, a bit of advice about how to approach the various medicine cabinets in this particular pharmacy: The techniques are meant to be fun. Experiment, play with them, look for things that appeal to you and try them out. Be sincere in your experimentation, but not serious. Not all techniques are for everybody, so Osho suggests to experiment with any given method for three to five days at first—that's usually enough time to feel whether it suits you and your particular temperament.

Sarito Carol Neiman, Editor

UNWINDING

~

Letting Go of Tension Through
Release and Relaxation

DIAGNOSIS

Consciousness cannot be against the body. Your consciousness is residing in the body, so they cannot be seen as inimical to each other. In every way, they are supportive of each other. I say something to you and my hand makes a gesture without my telling the hand. There is a deep synchronicity between me and my hand.

You walk, you eat, you drink, and all these things indicate that you are a body and consciousness as an organic whole. You cannot torture the body and raise your consciousness. The body has to be loved—you have to be a great friend. It is your home, you have to clean it of all junk, and you have to remember that it is in your service continuously, day in, day out. Even when you are asleep, your body is continuously working for you—digesting, changing your food into blood, taking out the dead cells from the body, bringing new oxygen, fresh oxygen, into the body—and you are fast asleep!

It is doing everything for your survival, for your life, although you are so ungrateful that you have never even thanked your body. On the contrary, your religions have been teaching you to torture it: "The body is your enemy and you have to get free from the body, its attachments."

I also know that you are more than the body and there is no need to have any attachment to it. But love is not an attachment; compassion is not an attachment. Love and compassion are absolutely needed for your body and its nourishment. And the better your body, the better the possibility for growing consciousness. It is an organic unity.

A totally new kind of education is needed in the world, where fundamentally everybody is introduced into the silences of the heart—in other words, meditations—and everybody has to be prepared to be compassionate to his or her own body. Because unless you are compassionate to your own body, you cannot be compassionate to any other body. It is a living organism, and it has done no harm to you. It has been continuously in service since you were conceived, and will be in your service till your death. It will do everything that you would like it to do, even the impossible, and it will not be disobedient to you.

It is inconceivable to create such a mechanism that is so obedient and so wise. If you become aware of all the functions of your body, you will be surprised. You have never thought about what your body has been doing. It is so miraculous, so mysterious. But you have never looked into it. You have never bothered to become acquainted with your own body—and you pretend to love other people? You cannot, because those other people also appear to you as bodies.

The body is the greatest mystery in the whole of existence. This mystery needs to be loved—its mysteries and its functioning need to be intimately inquired into.

The religions have unfortunately been absolutely against the body. But this antagonism is a clue, a definite indication that if a man learns the wisdom of the body and the mystery of the body, he will never bother about the priest or about God. He will have found the most mysterious within himself, and within the mystery of the body is the very shrine of your consciousness.

Once you have become aware of your consciousness, of your being, there is no God above you. Only such a person can be respectful toward other human beings, other living beings, because they all are as mysterious as he himself is—but different expressions, varieties, all of which make life richer. And once a man has found consciousness in himself, he has found the key to the ultimate. Any education that does not teach you to love your body, does not teach you to be compassionate to your body, does not teach you how to enter into its mysteries, will not be able to teach you how to enter into your own consciousness.

The body is the door—the body is the stepping-stone.

PRESCRIPTIONS

➤ DISSOLVING THE ARMOR

You carry armor around you. It is just armor—it is not clinging to you, *you* are clinging to *it*. So when you become aware of it, you can simply drop it. The armor is dead: if you don't carry it, it will disappear. Not only are you carrying it, you are also nourishing and feeding it continuously.

Every child is fluid. He has no frozen parts in him; the whole body is one organic unity. The head is not important and the feet are not unimportant. In fact, division doesn't exist; there are no demarcations. But by and by demarcations start coming up. Then the head becomes the master, the boss, and the whole body is divided into parts. A few parts are accepted by the society and a few parts are not. A few parts are dangerous for the society and have to be almost destroyed. That creates the whole problem.

So you have to watch where you feel limitations in the body.

Just do three things. The first thing: While you are walking or sitting, or whenever you are not doing anything, exhale deeply. The emphasis should be on exhalation, not on inhalation. So exhale deeply—as much air as you can throw out, throw. Exhale through the mouth, but do it slowly so it takes time. The longer it takes, the better, because then it goes deeper. When all the air inside the body is thrown out, then the body inhales; don't *you* inhale. The exhalation should be slow and deep and the inhalation should be fast. This will change the armor near the chest.

The second thing: If you can start a little running, that will be helpful. Not many miles—just one mile will do. Just visualize that a load is disappearing from the legs, as if it is falling off them. Legs carry the armor if your freedom has been restricted too much; if you have been told to do this and not to do that; to be this and not to be that; to go here and not to go there. So start running, and while running, also put more attention on exhalation. Once you regain your legs and their fluidity, you will have a tremendous energy flow.

The third thing: In the night when you go to sleep, take off your clothes and, while taking them off, just imagine that you are taking off not only your clothes, you are taking off your armor, too. Actually do it. Take it off and have a good deep breath—and then go to sleep as if unarmored, with nothing on the body and no restriction.

➤ FREE-FALL

Every night sit in a chair and let your head fall back, relaxed and at rest. You can use a pillow so you are in a resting posture and there is no tension in the neck. Then release your lower jaw—just relax it so the mouth opens slightly—and start breathing through the mouth, not through the nose. But the breathing should not be changed; it has to be as it is—natural. The first few breaths will be a little hectic. By and by the breathing will settle down and it will become very shallow. It will go in and out very slightly; that's how it should be. Keep the mouth open, eyes closed, and rest.

Then start feeling that your legs are becoming loose, as if they are being taken away from you, broken loose at the joints. Feel as if they are being taken away from you—they have been cut loose—and then start thinking that you are just the upper part of your body. The legs are gone.

Then the arms: think that both arms are becoming loose and being taken away from you. You may even be able to hear just a *click!* inside when they break away. You are no longer your arms; they are dead, taken away.

Then start thinking about the head—that it is being taken away, that you are being beheaded and that the head has broken away. Then leave it loose: wherever it turns—right or left—you cannot do anything. Just leave it loose; it has been taken away.

Then you have just your torso. Feel that you are only this much—this chest and the belly, that's all.

Do this for at least twenty minutes and then go to sleep. This is to be done just before sleep. Do it for at least three weeks.

Your restlessness will settle. Taking these parts as separate, only the essential will remain, so your whole energy will move in the essential part. That essential part will relax, and the energy will start flowing in your legs, in your arms, and in your head again, this time in a more proportionate way.

➤ THROAT CLEARING

If from your very childhood your expressiveness has not been as it should be—you have not been able to say what you wanted to say, you have not been able to do what you wanted to do—that unexpressed energy gets caught in the throat. The throat is the center of expression: it is not only the center of swallowing things, it is the center of expressing things. But many people use the throat center only for swallowing things. That is half its use, and the other half, the more important, remains starved.

So there are a few things to do if you need to become more expressive.

If you love a person, say the things that you want to say, even if they seem foolish; sometimes it is good to be foolish. Say the things that on the spur of the moment are born in you; don't hold them back. If you love a person, then go totally into it; don't remain controlled. If you are angry and you want to say something, then say it really hotly! Only cold anger is evil—hot anger, never—because cold anger is really dangerous. And that's what has been taught to people: remain cold even when you are angry, but then that poison will remain in your system. It is sometimes good to shout and so on and so forth, with every emotion.

.   .   .

Every night, just sit and just start swaying. The swaying has to be done in such a way that when you move to one side, one buttock touches the ground or the floor—so sit on something hard—and when you move to the other side, then the other buttock touches the ground. Only one should touch at one time, not both together.

This is one of the very ancient methods to hit the energy from the base of the spine.

If something is there in the throat, some energy is there and you have become capable of controlling this much energy, more of a flood is needed. It is so that your control becomes less and the energy is more, and you cannot control it, so the dam bursts. Do it for fifteen to twenty minutes.

After ten minutes of this exercise, just sway and start saying "Allah . . . Allah . . ." Say "Allah" when you go to one side, then "Allah" when you go to the other side. By and by you will feel more energy coming and the "Allah" will become louder and louder. A point will come after ten minutes when you will be almost shouting "Allah!" You will start perspiring; the energy will be coming so hot and the "Allah! Allah!" will become almost mad. When the dam is broken one goes mad.

Those two words are very good—they have the same letters! If you read it in one direction, the word is *dam*, and if you read it from the other, it is *mad*.

You will enjoy it. It will be weird but you will enjoy it! Then you can do it twice—in the morning, too: twenty minutes in the morning and twenty minutes in the evening.

➤ RELAX THE BELLY

Whenever you go in the morning to empty your bowels, afterward take a dry towel, a rough towel, and rub your belly. Pull the belly in and rub hard. Start at the right corner and go around really hard—go just around the navel but don't touch the navel— so that it gives you a good massage. Pull the belly in so all the intestines are massaged. Do it whenever you go for a bowel movement—up to twice or three times a day.

The second thing: In the daytime, between sunrise and sunset—never in the night—breathe as deeply as you can, as many times as you can. The more you breathe, the better, and the deeper you breathe, the better. But remember only one thing: breathing should happen from the belly and not from the chest, so that when you breathe in, the stomach goes up—not the chest. When you breathe in, the stomach goes out, and when you breathe out, the stomach goes in. Leave the chest as if it has nothing to do with it. Just breathe from the belly, so the whole day it will be like a subtle massage.

Watch a small child breathing . . . that's the right and natural way of breathing. The belly goes up and down and the chest remains completely unaffected by the passage of air. His whole energy is concentrated near his navel.

By and by we lose contact with the navel. We become more and more hung up in the head and the breathing becomes shallow. So whenever you remember during the day, take the breath in as deeply as possible—but let the belly be used.

Everybody breathes correctly in sleep because the interfering mind is not there. The belly goes up and down and breathing automatically becomes deep; you need not force it to become deep. Simply remain natural and it becomes deep. Depth is a consequence of its being natural.

⟶ DANCE LIKE A TREE

Go into the open if it is possible, stand amongst the trees, become a tree, and let the wind pass through you.

To feel identified with a tree is immensely strengthening and nourishing. One easily enters the primal consciousness; trees are still in it. Talk with trees and hug them. If it is not possible to go out, then just stand in the middle of the room, visualize yourself as a tree—it is raining and there is a strong wind—and start dancing. But dance as a tree and you will be able to get the flow.

It is only a question of learning the art of how to keep the energy flowing. This will be your key: you can always unlock it whenever it becomes locked.

⟶ TENSE FIRST, THEN RELAX INTO SLEEP

Every night before you go to sleep, stand in the middle of the room—exactly in the middle—and make your body as stiff and as tense as possible, almost as if you will burst. Do this for two minutes and then relax for two minutes, standing up. Do this tensing and relaxing two or three times and then just go to sleep.

So the whole body has to be made as tense as possible. Afterward, don't do anything else, so the whole night that relaxation goes deeper and deeper in you.

⬎ SOUNDLESS SILENCE

There is a silence that comes only when you are absolutely uncontrolled; it descends on you. So you have to remember this—that through your control you will be distracting your energy. The mind is a great dictator; it tries to control everything. And if it cannot control something, it denies it; it says it exists not.

Do this meditation every night before you go to sleep. Just sit in the bed, put the lights off—and be finished with anything that you want to do, because after the meditation you have simply to go into sleep. Then don't do anything; the "doer" should not be allowed after the meditation. Simply relax and move into sleep, because sleep also comes—you cannot control it. There is one quality in sleep that is almost like meditation— silence –in that it simply comes. That's why many people are suffering from insomnia; they are trying to control even that, hence the problem. It is nothing that you can do anything about. You can simply wait; you can simply be in a relaxed, receptive mood.

So after this meditation you have simply to relax and go into sleep so that there will be continuity, and the meditation will go on flowing in you. The whole night the vibration will be there. You will feel in the morning when you open your eyes that you have slept in a totally different way. There has been a qualitative change; it was not just sleep. Something else, deeper than sleep, was present. You have been showered by something and you don't know what it is and how to categorize it.

The meditation is very simple. Sit in the bed, relax the body, close the eyes, and just imagine that you are lost in a mountainous region. It is a dark night, there is no moon in the sky, and it is a very clouded sky. You cannot see even a single star—it is absolutely dark—and you cannot see even your own hand. You are lost in the mountains and it is very difficult to find your way. There is every danger; any moment you can fall into some valley, into some abyss, and you will be gone forever. So you are groping very cautiously. You are fully alert because the danger is tremendous, and when the danger is tremendous one has to be very alert.

The imagining of the dark night and the mountainous region is just to create a very dangerous situation. And you are very alert; even if a pin drops, you will be able to hear it. Then suddenly you come near a precipice. One can feel that now there is no way ahead and one never knows how deep the abyss is. So you take a rock and throw it into the abyss, just to see how deep it is.

Wait and listen for the report of the rock falling on other rocks. Go on listening, go on listening, go on listening. But there is no report—it is as if it is an abyss with no bottom. Just through your continuing to listen, a great fear arises in you, and with that fear of course your awareness becomes a flame.

Let it be actually your imagination. You throw the rock and you wait. You go on and on listening; you wait with a beating heart and no sound. It is utterly silent. In that silence, fall asleep. In that soundless silence, fall asleep.

⟶ ENERGY FLOW

Energy always flows toward the object of love.

So whenever you feel energy stuck anywhere, that is the secret to make it flow. Find an object of love. Any object will do; that is just an excuse. If you can touch a tree very lovingly, the energy will start flowing, because wherever love is, energy pours toward that. It is just like water flowing downward, so wherever the sea is, the water seeks the sea level and goes on moving.

Wherever there is love, energy seeks the "love level"—it goes on moving.

Massage can help; if you do it very lovingly it can help. But anything can help.

Take a rock in your hand with deep love and with a deep concern. Close your eyes and feel tremendous love for the rock—grateful that the rock exists and grateful that it accepts your love. Suddenly you will see: there is a pulsation and the energy is moving. Then by and by there is no need to have any object, really—just the idea that you love somebody and energy will be flowing. Then even the idea can be dropped; just be loving and energy will be flowing.

Love is flow, and whenever we are frozen it is because we don't love.

Love is warmth, and the frozenness cannot happen if the warmth is there. When love is not there, everything is cold. You start falling below the zero point.

So one of the very important things to remember: love is warm, so is hate; indifference is cold. So sometimes even when you hate, energy starts flowing. Of course that flow is destructive. In anger, energy starts flowing—that's why people feel somehow good after anger; something was released. It is very destructive; it could have been creative if it had been released through love, but it is better than not being released.

If you are indifferent, you don't flow. So anything that melts you and warms you up is good. It is not massage that works, it is your concern, your love. Now try the same thing on a rock: just massage the rock and see what happens. And be loving. Try it on a tree; when you feel that it is happening just sit silently and try. Remember somebody or something you love—a man, a woman, a child, or a flower. Remember that flower—just the idea—and suddenly you will see that energy is flowing.

Then drop that idea, too. One day simply sit silently just being loving—not addressed, not to anybody in particular. In a loving mood just sit silently and lovingly and you will see that it is flowing. Then you know the key. Love is the key. Love is the flow.

➤ RECHANNELING SEX ENERGY

Sit straight—on a chair or on the floor—with the spine straight but loose and not tense.

Inhale slowly and deeply. Don't be in a hurry; very slowly go on inhaling. The belly comes up first; you go on inhaling. The chest comes up next and then finally you can feel that the body is filled with air up to the neck. Then for a moment or two just keep the breath in, for as long as you can without straining, then exhale. Exhale also very slowly but in the reverse order. When the belly is being emptied, pull it in so that all the air goes out. This has to be done just seven times.

Then sit silently and start repeating "Om . . . om . . . om." While repeating "om," keep your concentration on the third eye spot between the two eyebrows. Forget about the breathing and go on repeating "Om . . . om . . . om . . ." in a very drowsy way, as a mother would sing a lullaby so her child goes to sleep. The mouth should be closed, so that the tongue is touching the roof of the mouth, and your whole concentration is on the third eye. Do this for just two or three minutes and you will feel that the whole head is relaxing. When it starts relaxing, you will immediately feel inside that a tightness is dropping, a tension is disappearing.

Then bring your concentration down to the throat; go on repeating "om" but with your concentration on the throat. Then you will see that your shoulders, your throat, and your face are relaxing and that the tension is falling away like a burden dropping; you are becoming weightless.

Then drop deeper, bringing your concentration to the navel and continuing the "om." You are going deeper and deeper and deeper. Then finally you come to the sex center. This will take about ten or fifteen minutes, so go slowly; there is no hurry.

When you have reached the sex center, the whole body will be relaxed and you will feel a glow as if some aura or some light is surrounding you. You are full of energy, but the energy is like a reservoir, full of energy but with no ripples. Then you can sit in that state as long as you like.

The meditation is over; now you are simply enjoying. Stop the "om" and simply sit. If you feel like it you can lie down, but if you change your position, the state will disappear sooner, so sit a little and enjoy it.

The whole point is that when your body becomes too tense for any reason at all, just do it and it will give you total relaxation.

⌒ NAIL-BITERS ANONYMOUS

When there is too much energy and you don't know what to do with it, you start biting your nails or smoking cigarettes. It is the same—biting the nails or smoking cigarettes. One starts doing anything just to remain engaged; otherwise the energy is there and it is too much to bear. When people condemn it, that "this is nervousness"—then more repression happens. You are not even free to bite your nails! The nails are yours and you are not even allowed to bite your nails. Then people find cunning ways—chewing gum. . . . Those are subtle ways: nobody will object too much. If you are smoking a cigarette, nobody will object too much. Now, biting the nails is less harmful—in fact not harmful at all. It is a harmless joy. It looks a little ugly and looks a little childish, that's all. And you are trying not to do it.

You have to learn to live more energetically, that's all, and all these things will disappear. Dance more, sing more, swim more, and go for long walks. Use your energy in creative ways. Move from the minimum to the maximum. Live life more intensely. If you are making love then make wild love, not just ladylike—that means at the minimum. A "lady" means one who lives at the minimum, or does not really live but only pretends to. Be wild! And now you are no longer a child, so you are allowed to be a nuisance in your own place. Jump and sing and jog.

Just try this for a few weeks and you will be surprised: nail-biting disappears on its own. Now you have far more interesting things to do—who bothers about the nails? But always look at the cause and never be too concerned with the symptom.

➤ JUST SAY YES!

"No" is our basic attitude. Why? Because with "no" you feel you are somebody. The mother feels she is somebody—she can say no. The child is negated, the child's ego is hurt, and the mother's ego is fulfilled. "No" is ego-fulfilling; it is food for the ego, which is why we train ourselves to say no.

Move anywhere in life and you will find no-sayers everywhere, because with "no" you feel your authority—you are *someone,* you can say no. To say "Yes, sir" makes you feel inferior; you feel that you are someone's subordinate, a nobody. Only then do you say "Yes, sir."

Yes is positive and no is negative.

Remember this: no is ego-fulfilling; yes is the method to discover the self. No is strengthening the ego; yes is destroying it.

First find out whether you can say yes. If you cannot say yes, if it is impossible to say yes, only then say no.

But our method is first to say no; if it is impossible to say no, only then, with a defeated attitude, do we say yes.

Try it someday. Take it as a vow that for twenty-four hours you will try in every situation to start with yes. Look what a deep relaxation it gives to you. Just ordinary things! The child asks to go to the movies. He *will* go; your no means nothing. On the contrary, your no becomes an invitation, your no becomes an attraction, because when you are strengthening your ego, the child is also trying to strengthen his. He will try to go against your no, and he knows ways to make your no a yes; he knows how to transform it. He knows it needs just a little effort, insistence, and your no becomes yes.

For twenty-four hours, try in every way to start with yes. You will feel much difficulty, because then you will become aware that immediately the no comes first! In anything the no comes first—that has become the habit. Don't use it; use yes, and then see how the yes relaxes you.

·   ·   ·

Right thinking means to start thinking with yes. It doesn't mean that you cannot use no; it only means to start with yes. Look with a yes-saying mind. And then, if it is impossible, say no. You will not find many points to say no if you start with yes. If you start with no, you will not find many points to say yes. The starting point means 90 percent is done. Your start colors everything, even the end. Right thinking means think, but think with a sympathetic mind. Think with a yes-saying mind.

⟶ LAUGH YOUR TROUBLES AWAY

Just sitting silently, create a giggle in the very guts of your being, as if your whole body is giggling or laughing. Start swaying with that laughter and let it spread from the belly to the whole of your body—hands laughing, feet laughing, go crazily into it. For twenty minutes do the laughing. If it comes uproariously, loudly, allow it. If it comes silently, then sometimes silently, sometimes loudly, allow it, but do twenty minutes of laughing.

Then lie down on the earth or on the floor; spread yourself on the floor, facing the floor. If it is warm and you can do it in the garden, on the ground, that will be far better. If it can be done naked, that will be even better. Make contact with the earth, the whole body lying down there on the earth, and just feel that the earth is the mother and you are the child. Get lost in that feeling.

Twenty minutes of laughter, then twenty minutes of earthing, a deep contact with the earth. Breathe with the earth and feel one with the earth. We come from the earth and one day we will be going back to it. After those twenty minutes of energizing—because the earth will give so much energy that your dancing will have a different quality to it—dance for twenty minutes . . . just any dance. Put music on and dance.

If the weather is bad, then you can do this inside a room. But when it is sunny do it outside, and if it is very cold, cover yourself with a blanket. Find ways and means but continue to do it, and within six to eight months you will see great changes happening on their own.

2

HEAD REMEDIES

~

Taming the Mind and
(on occasion)Dropping Out of It

DIAGNOSIS

The mind is simply a biocomputer. When the child is born he has no mind; there is no chattering going on in him. It takes almost three to four years for his mechanism to start functioning. And you will see that girls start talking earlier than boys. They are bigger chatterboxes! They have a better-quality biocomputer.

It needs information to be fed into it; that's why if you try to remember your life backward, you will get stuck somewhere at the age of four if you are a man, or at the age of three if you are a woman. Beyond that is a blank. You were there; many things must have happened, many incidents must have occurred, but there seems to be no memory being recorded, so you cannot remember. But you can remember back to the age of four or three very clearly.

The mind collects its data from the parents, from the school, from other children, neighbors, relatives, society, churches . . . all around there are sources. And you must have seen little children, when they start speaking for the first time, repeating the same word over and over. The joy! A new mechanism has started functioning in them.

When they can make sentences, they will make sentences so joyously, again and again. When they start asking questions they will ask about each and every thing. They are not interested in your answers, remember! Watch a child when he asks a question; he is not interested in your answer, so please don't give him a long answer from the *Encyclopaedia Britannica*. The child is not interested in your answer; the child is simply enjoying that he can question. A new faculty has come into being in him.

And this is how he goes on collecting; then he will start reading . . . and more words. And in this society, silence does not pay; words pay, and the more articulate you are, the more you will be paid. What are your leaders? What are your politicians? What are your professors? What are your priests, theologians, philosophers, condensed to one thing? They are very articulate. They know how to use words meaningfully, significantly, consistently, so that they can impress people.

It is rarely taken note of that our whole society is dominated by verbally articulate people. They may not know anything; they may not be wise; they may not even be intelligent. But one thing is certain: they know how to play with words. It is a game, and they have learned it. And it pays in respectability, in money, in power— in every way. So everybody tries, and the mind becomes filled with many words, many thoughts.

And you can turn any computer on or off—but you cannot turn the mind off. The switch does not exist. There is no reference that when God made the world, when he made man, he made a switch for the mind so that you could turn it on or turn it off. There is no switch, so from birth to death it continues.

You will be surprised that the people who understand computers and who understand the human brain have a very strange idea.

If we take out the brain from the skull of a human being and keep it alive artificially, it goes on chattering in the same way. It does not matter to it that it is now no longer connected to the poor person who was suffering from it; it still dreams. Now that it is connected to machines, it still dreams, it still imagines, it still fears, it still projects, hopes, tries to be this or that. And it is completely unaware that now it can do nothing; the person it used to be attached to is no longer there. You can keep this brain alive for thousands of years attached to mechanical devices, and it will go on chattering, round and round—the same things, because we have not yet been able to teach it new things. Once we can teach it new things, it will repeat new things.

There is an idea prevalent in scientific circles that it is a great waste that a man like Albert Einstein dies and his brain dies with him. If we could save the brain, implant the brain into somebody else's body, then the brain would go on functioning. It doesn't matter whether Albert Einstein is alive or not; that brain will continue to think about the theory of relativity, about stars, and about theoretical physics. The idea is that just as people donate blood and people choose to donate their eyes after they die, people should start donating their brains, too, so that their brains can be kept. If we feel that they are special brains, highly qualified and a sheer waste to let them die, then we can transplant them.

Some idiot can be made an Albert Einstein, and the idiot will never know, because inside the skull of man there is no sensitivity; you can change anything and the person will never know. Just make the person unconscious and change anything you want to change in his brain—you can change the whole brain—and he will wake up with the new brain, with the new chattering, and he will not even suspect what has happened.

This chattering is our education, and it is basically wrong because it teaches you only half of the process—how to use the mind. It does not teach you how to stop it so that it can relax—because even when you are asleep it goes on continuing. It knows no sleep. Seventy years, eighty years, it has worked continuously.

But it is possible to put a switch on the mind and turn it off when it is not needed—we call it meditation. It is helpful in two ways: it will give you a peace, a silence, which you have never known before, and it will give you an acquaintance with yourself that, because of the chattering mind, is not possible now. It has always kept you engaged.

Secondly, it will also give the mind rest. And if we can give the mind rest, it will be more capable of doing things more efficiently, more intelligently.

So on both sides—on the side of the mind and on the side of your being—you will be benefited; you just have to learn how to stop the mind from functioning, how to say to it, "That's enough; now go to sleep. I am awake, don't be worried."

Use the mind when it is needed—and then it is fresh, young, full of energy and juice. Then whatever you say is not just dry bones; it is full of life, full of authority, full of truth and sincerity, and has tremendous meaning. You may be using the same words, but now the mind has collected so much power by resting that each word it uses becomes afire, becomes filled with power.

What is known in the world as charisma is simply a mind that knows how to relax and let energy collect. So when it speaks it is poetry; when it speaks it is gospel; when it speaks it need not give any evidence or any logic—just its own energy is enough to influence people. And people have always known that there *is* something, although they have never been able to exactly pinpoint what it is that they have called charisma.

I am telling you what charisma is because I know it from my own experience. A mind that is working day and night is bound to become weak, dull, unimpressive, somehow dragging. At the most it is utilitarian. You go to purchase vegetables—it is helpful. But more than that it has no power. So millions of people who could have been charismatic remain poor and unimpressive, without any authority and without any power.

If it is possible—and it *is* possible—to put the mind to silence and use it only when it is needed, then it comes with a rushing force. It has gathered so much energy that each word uttered goes directly to your heart.

People think that these minds of charismatic personalities are hypnotic; they are not hypnotic. They are really so powerful, so fresh . . . it is always spring.

This is for the mind. For the being, the silence opens up a new universe of eternity, of deathlessness, of all that you can think of as blessing, as benediction. Hence my insistence that meditation is the essential religion—the only religion. Nothing else is needed. Everything else is nonessential ritual.

Meditation is just the essence, the very essence. You cannot cut anything out of it.

And it gives you both worlds. It gives you the other world—the divine, the world of godliness—and it gives you this world, too. Then you are not poor. You have a richness—but not of money. There are many kinds of richness, and the man who is rich because of money is the lowest as far as the categories of richness are concerned. Let me say it in this way: the man of wealth is the poorest rich man. Looked at from the side of the poor, he is the richest poor man. Looked at from the side of a creative artist, of a dancer, of a musician, of a scientist, he is the poorest rich man. And as far as the world of ultimate awakening is concerned, he cannot even be called rich.

Meditation will make you ultimately rich by giving you the world of your innermost being. And also relatively rich, because it will release your powers of mind into certain talents that you have.

My own experience is that everybody is born with a certain talent, and unless he lives that talent to its fullest, something in him will remain missing. He will go on feeling that somehow something is not there that should be.

Give the mind a rest—it needs it! And it is so simple: just become a witness to it. And it will give you both things.

Slowly, slowly, the mind starts learning to be silent. And once it knows that by being silent it becomes powerful, then its words are not just words; they have a validity and a richness and a quality that they never had before—so much so that they go directly, like arrows. They bypass the logical barriers and reach to the very heart.

Then the mind is a good servant of immense power in the hands of silence.

Then the being is the master, and the master can use the mind whenever it is needed and can switch it off whenever it is not needed.

PRESCRIPTIONS

⟿ ENJOY THE MIND

Don't try to stop the mind. It is a very natural part of you; you will go crazy if you try to stop it. It will be like a tree trying to stop its leaves; the tree will go mad. The leaves are very natural to it.

So the first thing: Don't try to stop your thinking; it's perfectly good.

The second thing: Just not stopping it will not be enough; the second is to enjoy it. Play with it! It is a beautiful game. Playing with it, enjoying it, welcoming it, you will start becoming more alert about it, more aware of it. But that awareness will come very, very indirectly; it will not be an effort to become aware. When you are *trying* to become aware, then the mind distracts you and you become angry with it. You feel that this is an ugly mind and it is constantly chattering; you want to be silent and it doesn't allow you, so you start feeling inimical toward the mind.

That's not good; that is dividing yourself into two. Then you and the mind become two, and conflict and friction start. All friction is suicidal because it is your energy being wasted unnecessarily. We don't have that much energy to waste in fighting with ourselves. The same energy has to be used in joy.

So start enjoying the thought process. Just see the nuances of thoughts, the turns they take, how one thing leads to another, how they get hooked into each other. It is really a miracle to watch! Just a small thought can take you to the farthest end, and if you look you don't see any connection.

Enjoy it—let it be a game. Play it deliberately and you will be surprised: sometimes just enjoying it, you will find beautiful pauses. Suddenly you will find that a dog is barking and nothing is arising in your mind, no chain of thinking starts. The dog goes on barking and you go on listening and no thought arises. Small gaps will arise . . . but they are not to be produced. They come on their own, and when they come, they are beautiful. In those small gaps you will start watching the watcher—but that will be natural. Again thoughts will start and you will enjoy it. Go on easily, take it easy. Awareness will come to you, but it will come indirectly.

Watching, enjoying, seeing thoughts taking their turn, is as beautiful as seeing the sea with millions of waves. This, too, is a sea, and thoughts are waves. But people go and enjoy the waves in the ocean and don't enjoy the waves in their consciousness.

➣ CHANGE THE MIND

Whenever you want to change a pattern of the mind that has become a long-standing habit, breathing is the best thing. All habits of the mind are associated with the pattern of breathing. Change the pattern of breathing and the mind changes immediately, instantly. Try it!

Whenever you see that a judgment is coming and you are getting into an old habit, immediately exhale—as if you are throwing the judgment out with the exhalation. Exhale deeply, pulling the stomach in, and as you throw out the air, feel or visualize that the whole judgment is being thrown out.

Then take in fresh air deeply, two or three times.

Just see what happens. You will feel a complete freshness; the old habit will not have been able to take possession.

So start with exhalation, not inhalation. When you want to take something in, start by inhaling; if you want to throw something out, start with an exhalation. Just see how immediately the mind is affected. Immediately you will see that the mind has moved somewhere else; a new breeze has come. You are not in the old groove, so you will not repeat the old habit.

This is true for all habits. For example, if you smoke, if the urge comes to smoke and you don't want to, immediately exhale deeply and throw the urge out. Have a fresh breath in and you will see immediately that the urge has gone. This can become a very, very important tool for inner change.

⌐ CHANT "OM"

Whenever you feel that there is too much disturbance around you, or your mind is distracted too much, just chant "om."

Make it a point for at least twenty minutes in the morning and twenty minutes in the evening to sit silently, in a comfortable posture, with your eyes half open looking downward. Breathing should be slow, and the body unmoving. Start chanting "om" inside; there is no need to bring it out. It will be more penetrating with your lips closed; even the tongue should not move. Repeat "om" quickly—"om om om om"— quickly and loudly but inside you. Just feel that it is vibrating all over the body from the feet to the head, from the head to the feet.

Each "om" falls into your consciousness like a rock thrown into a pool. Ripples arise and spread to the very end. The ripples go on expanding and touch the whole body.

Doing this, there will be moments—and they will be the most beautiful moments—when you will not be repeating anything and everything has stopped. Suddenly you will become aware that you are not chanting and everything has stopped. Enjoy it. If thoughts start coming, again start chanting.

When you do it at night, do it at least two hours before you go to sleep. Otherwise, if you do it just before you go to bed, you will not be able to go to sleep because it will make you so fresh that you will not feel like it. You will feel as if it is morning and you have rested well, so what is the point of sleeping?

Do it quickly, but you can find your own pace. After two or three days you will find what suits you. It suits a few people to do it very fast—"om om om," almost overlapping. Others it suits to do it very slowly. So it depends on you. Whatever feels good, continue.

➤ WATCH OUT FOR THE "NO"

The mind always functions negatively. The very function of the mind is to negate, to say no.

Just watch yourself and how many times you say no during the day, and reduce that quota. Watch yourself and how many times you say yes—increase that quota.

By and by you will see just a slight change in the degrees of yes and no, and your personality is changing basically. Watch how many times you say no where yes would have been easier, where there was really no need to say no. Watch how many times you could have said yes but either you said no or you kept quiet.

Whenever you say yes, it goes against the ego. The ego cannot eat yes; it feeds itself on noes. Say "No! No! No!" and a great ego arises within you.

Just go to the railway station: you may be alone at the window to purchase a ticket, but the clerk will start doing something; he will not look at you. He is trying to say no. He will at least make you wait. He will pretend that he is very busy; he will look into this register and that. He will force you to wait. That gives a feeling of power, that he is no ordinary clerk—he can make anybody wait.

The first thing that comes to your mind is "no." "Yes" is almost difficult. You say yes only when you feel absolutely helpless and you *have* to say it. Just watch it! Make yourself a yea-sayer; drop nay-saying, because it is the poison of "no" on which the ego feeds itself, nourishes itself.

➤ MOVE FROM THE HEAD TO THE HEART

Feeling is real life. Thinking is phony because thinking is always *about;* it is never the real thing. It is not thinking about the wine that can make you intoxicated, it *is* the wine. You can go on thinking about the wine, but just by thinking about the wine you will never become intoxicated. You will have to drink it, and the drinking happens through feeling.

Thinking is a pseudo-activity, a substitute activity. It gives you a false sense of something happening, and nothing happens. So shift from thinking to feeling, and the best way will be to start breathing from the heart.

During the day, as many times as you remember, just take a deep breath. Feel it hitting just in the middle of the chest. Feel as if the whole existence is pouring into you, into the place where your heart center is. It differs with different people; ordinarily it is leaning to the right. It has nothing to do with the physical heart. It is a totally different thing; it belongs to the subtle body.

Breathe deeply, and whenever you do, do it at least five times with deep breaths. Take the breath in and fill the heart. Just feel it in the middle, that existence is pouring in through the heart. Vitality, life, the divine, nature—everything pouring in.

Then exhale deeply, again from the heart, and feel you are pouring all that has been given to you back into the divine, into existence.

Do it many times during the day, but whenever you do it, do five breaths at once. That will help you to shift from the head to the heart.

You will become more and more sensitive, more and more

aware of many things of which you have not been aware. You will smell more; you will taste more; you will touch more. You will see more and you will hear more; everything will become intense. So move from the head to the heart and all your senses will become suddenly luminous. You will start feeling life really throbbing in you, ready to jump and ready to flow.

⚊ SOUND ADVICE

There is a blissful sound constantly inside you, as there is inside everybody. We just have to be silent to hear it. Because the head is too noisy, it cannot hear the still, small voice of the heart, and it *is* a very small, still voice. Unless all is quiet you never hear it, but it is the link between you and existence. Once you have heard it, you know from where you are joined, linked, bridged to existence. Once you have heard it, it becomes very easy to go into it. Then you can concentrate on it and easily slip into it. And whenever you go into it, it rejuvenates you; it gives you tremendous strength and makes you alive again and again.

If a person can go into this inner sound again and again, he never loses track of the divine; he can live in the world and can remain in contact with the divine. By and by the knack is learned and then even in the marketplace you can go on hearing it. Once you know it is there, it is not difficult to hear it. Then the whole noise of the world cannot prevent you from hearing it. The problem is only to hear it for the first time, because you don't know where it is or what it is and how to allow it.

All that is needed is to become more and more silent.

Sit in silence. Whenever you have time, just for one hour every day, don't do anything—sit and listen. Listen to the sounds all around, with no particular purpose, with no interpretation as to what they mean. Just listen for no reason at all. A sound is there, so one has to listen.

Slowly, slowly, the mind starts becoming silent. The sound is heard but the mind is no longer interpreting it—no longer appreciating it and no longer thinking about it. Suddenly the gestalt changes. When the mind is silent, listening to the outer sound, suddenly a new sound is heard that is not from the outside but from the inside. And once you have heard it, the thread is in your hands.

Just follow that thread, go deeper and deeper into it. There is a very deep well in your being, and those who know how to go into it live in a totally different world, in a separate reality.

⟶ GEAR SHIFT

One should continually change one's activities, because the brain has many centers. For example, if you do mathematics, then a certain part of the brain functions and the other parts rest. Then you read poetry—and the part that was functioning in mathematics rests and another part starts functioning.

That's why in universities and schools we change periods after forty or forty-five minutes—because each center of the brain has the capacity to function for forty minutes. Then it feels tired and needs a rest, and the best rest is to change the work so that some other center starts working and one relaxes. So continual change is very, very good; it enriches you.

Ordinarily, you do a thing and the mind becomes obsessed; you go after it madly. But that's bad; one should not become so possessed while doing anything. Become absorbed but always remain a master; otherwise you will become a slave, and slavery is not good. Even slavery to meditation is not good. If you can't stop doing a certain thing or you stop only very reluctantly, that simply shows that you don't know how to change gears in the mind.

So do one thing:

Whenever you are doing something and you want to do something else, stop and for five minutes simply exhale as deeply as possible. For example, if you are meditating and want to do something else, after you stop meditating, exhale deeply for five minutes. Then let the body inhale; don't *you* inhale. Have a feeling that you are throwing out everything that was in the mind, in the body, and in the rest of your system. Just do this for five minutes, then start doing some other work. Immediately you will feel you have changed.

You need to be in a neutral gear for five minutes. If you want to change gear in a car, you must first shift to neutral—even if it is just for a single moment, you must be in neutral. The more efficient the driver, the faster he can move from neutral. So give five minutes to the neutral gear, where you are not working at anything—just breathing, just being. Then by and by you can go on reducing the length of time. After one month, do it for just four minutes; after two months, just three minutes, and so on.

By and by there will come a point where just one exhalation is enough and you are finished with the work—it is closed, there is a full stop—and then you can start other work.

➤ FROM HEAD TO HEART TO BEING

Man can function from three centers: one is the head, another is the heart, and the third is the navel. If you function from the head, you will go on spinning more and more thoughts. They are very insubstantial, dream-stuff; they promise much and they deliver nothing.

The mind is a great cheat! But it has tremendous capacities to delude you because it can project. It can give you great utopias, great desires, and it always goes on saying, "Tomorrow it is going to happen"—and it never happens! Nothing ever happens in the head. The head is not the place for anything to happen.

The second center is the heart. It is the center for feeling—one feels through the heart. You are closer to home; not home yet, but closer. When you feel, you are more substantial; you have more solidity. When you feel, there is a possibility that something may happen. There is no possibility with the head; there is a small possibility with the heart.

But the real thing is not even the heart. The real thing is deeper than the heart, which is the navel. It is the center of being.

Thinking, feeling, and being—these are the three centers.

Feel more and then you will think less. Don't fight with thinking because fighting with thinking is again creating other thoughts, of fighting. Then the mind is never defeated. If you win, it is the mind that has won; if you are defeated, *you* are defeated. Either way, you are defeated, so never fight with thoughts. It is futile.

Rather than fighting with thoughts, move your energy into feeling. Sing rather than think; love rather than philosophize; read poetry rather than prose. Dance, look at nature, and whatever you do, do it through the heart.

For example, if you touch somebody, touch the person from your heart. Touch feelingly; let your being vibrate. When you look at somebody, don't just look with stone-dead eyes. Pour out your energy through your eyes and immediately you will see that something is happening in the heart. It is only a question of trying.

The heart is the neglected center. Once you start paying attention to it, it starts functioning. When it starts functioning, the energy that was moving in the mind automatically starts moving through the heart. And the heart is closer to the energy center—the energy center is in the navel—so to pump energy to the head is hard work, in fact.

So start feeling more and more. This is the first step. Once you have taken this step, the second will be very, very easy. First, love—half the journey is complete. And as it is easy to move from the head to the heart, it is even easier to move from the heart to the navel.

In the navel you are simply a being, a pure being—no feeling and no thinking. You are not moving at all. That is the center of the cyclone.

Everything else is moving: the head is moving, the heart is moving, and the body is moving. Everything is moving; everything is in constant flux. Only the center of your existence, the navel center, is unmoving; it is the hub of the wheel.

⤳ TIME OUT

Every day for at least one hour, sit silently anywhere. Go to the river or to the garden, somewhere where nobody is disturbing you. Relax the muscles of the body, don't strain, and with closed eyes tell the mind, "Now, go on! Do whatever you want to do. I will witness and I will watch."

You will be surprised: for a few moments you will see that the mind is not working at all. For a few moments, sometimes just for a second, you will see that the mind is not working and in that gap you will have a feel of reality as it is, without your imagination always functioning. But it will be only for a moment, a very small moment, and then the mind will start working again.

When the mind starts working and thoughts start running and images start floating, you will not become aware of it immediately. Only later on, after a few minutes, will you become aware that the mind is working and you have lost your way. Then again hold your attention; tell the mind, "Now, go on and I will be just a witness," and again the mind will stop for a second.

Those seconds are tremendously valuable. Those are the first moments of reality, the first glimpses of reality, the first windows. They are very small, just small gaps, and they come and go, but in those moments you will start having the taste of reality.

Slowly, slowly, by and by, you will see that those intervals become bigger and bigger. They will happen only when you are tremendously alert.

When you are tremendously alert the mind does not function, because the attention itself functions like a light in a dark room. When the light is there, darkness is not there. When you are present, the mind is absent—your presence is the mind's absence. When you are not present, the mind starts functioning. Your absence is the mind's presence.

➤ CONFUSION CLEARING

Let confusion be there. Don't try to sort things out, don't try to figure things out, because whatever you do is not going to help now. Simply watch.

One meditation you can start every night before you go to sleep. Just sit in your bed—sit in a relaxed way—and close your

eyes and feel the body relaxing. If the body starts leaning forward, allow it; it may lean forward. It may like to take a womb
posture, just as when a child is in the mother's womb. If you
feel like that, just move into the womb posture. Become a small
child in the mother's womb.

Then just listen to your breathing, nothing else. Just listen
to it—the breathing going in and the breathing going out; the
breathing going in and the breathing going out. I'm not saying
to verbalize it—just feel it going in; when it is going out, feel it
going out. Just feel it, and in that feeling you will feel tremendous silence and clarity arising.

This is just for ten to twenty minutes—a minimum of ten
minutes, a maximum of twenty—then go to sleep.

Just let things happen as if you are not the doer.

⟜ Unleash the Inner Chatterbox

If a continuous internal dialogue is there, it must have a cause
inside. Rather than repressing it, allow it.

Through allowing it, it will disappear. It wants to communicate something to you. Your mind wants to talk to you.
Something you have not been listening to, not caring about,
have been indifferent to, wants to relate to you. You may not be
aware of what it wants to relate because you have always been
fighting and thinking it is crazy, trying to stop it or convert it
into something else. All diversions are a sort of repression.

⟜

Do one thing. Every night before you go to sleep, for forty
minutes sit facing the wall and start talking—talk loudly. Enjoy

it and be with it. If you find that there are two voices, then talk from both sides. Give your support to this side, then answer from the other side, and see how you can create a beautiful dialogue.

Don't try to manipulate it, because you are not saying it for anybody. If it is going to be crazy, let it be. Don't try to cut anything out or censor anything, because then the whole point is lost.

Do it for at least ten days, and for those forty minutes, in no way try to be against it. Just put your whole energy into it. Within ten days something will surface that has been trying to tell you something but you have not been listening, or there will be something of which you were aware but didn't want to hear. Listen to it and then it is finished.

Start this talking to the wall and be totally in it. Keep the lights either off or very dim. If sometimes you feel like shouting and becoming angry in your talk, become angry and shout, because it will go deep only when it is done with feeling. If you are just on a head trip and you go on repeating words like a dead tape, that won't help and the real thing won't surface.

Talk with feeling and with gestures, as if the other is present there. After about twenty-five minutes you will warm up. The last fifteen minutes will be tremendously beautiful; you will enjoy it. After ten days you will see that by and by the inner talk is disappearing and you have come to understand a few things you have never understood about yourself.

➤ THE 24-DAY DECISION

A decision is good when it comes out of life; it is bad when it comes only out of the head. When it comes only out of the head it is never decisive; it is always a conflict. The alternatives remain open and the mind goes on and on, from this side to that. That's how the mind creates conflict.

The body is always herenow and the mind is never herenow; that is the whole conflict. You breathe here and now; you cannot breathe tomorrow and you cannot breathe yesterday. You have to breathe this moment. But you can *think* about tomorrow and you can *think* about yesterday. So the body remains in the present and the mind goes on hopping between past and future. There is a split between body and mind. The body is in the present and the mind is never in the present; they never meet, they never come across each other. Because of that split, anxiety, anguish, and tension arise; one is tense—this tension is worry.

The mind has to be brought to the present, because there is no other time.

So whenever you start thinking of the future and the past too much, just relax and pay attention to your breathing. Every day for at least one hour, just sit in a chair, relaxed, make yourself comfortable, and close your eyes. Just start looking at the breathing. Don't change it; just look, watch. By your watching it, it will become slower and slower and slower. If ordinarily you take eight breaths in one minute, you will start taking six, then five, four, three, and then two. Within two or three weeks you will be taking one breath per minute. When you are taking one breath per minute, the mind is coming closer to the body.

Out of this small meditation a time comes when for minutes the breathing stops. Three or four minutes pass and then one breath. Then you are in tune with the body and you will know for the first time what the present is. Otherwise it is just a word; the mind has never known it, the mind has never experienced it. It knows the past and it knows the future, so when you say "the present," the mind understands something in between past and future, in between something, but the mind has no experience of it.

So for twenty-four days, for one hour every day, relax into breathing and let the breathing go on; it goes on automatically. When you walk it goes on automatically. Slowly, slowly, there will be gaps and those gaps will give you the first experience of the present. Out of these twenty-four, twenty-five days, suddenly a decision will arise.

It is immaterial what decision comes up. The most important thing is from where it comes—not *what* it is but *from where*. If it comes from the head it will create misery. But if some decision arises from your totality, then you never, ever repent for a single moment. A man who lives in the present knows nothing of repentance; he never looks back. He never changes his past and his memories, and he never arranges his future.

A decision from the head is an ugly thing. The very word *decision* comes from the Latin "to cut off"; it cuts you off. It is not a good word. It simply means it cuts you off from reality. The head continuously cuts you off from reality.

3

THE ART OF THE HEART

~

Nourishing Your Love Potential

DIAGNOSIS

We have become too much obsessed with the head. Our whole education, our whole civilization, is obsessed with the head because the head has made all kinds of technological advances; we think that's all.

What can the heart give to us? True; it cannot give you great technology; it cannot give you great industry; it cannot give you money. It can give you joy; it can give you celebration. It can give you a tremendous feeling for beauty, for music, for poetry. It can guide you into the world of love, and ultimately into the world of prayer, but those things are not commodities. You cannot grow your bank balance through the heart; and you cannot fight great wars, and you cannot make atom bombs and hydrogen bombs, and you cannot destroy people through the heart. The heart knows only how to create and the head knows only how to destroy. The head is destructive, and our whole education has become trapped in the head.

Our universities, our colleges, our schools, are all destroying humanity. They think they are serving but they are simply fooling themselves. Unless man becomes balanced, unless the heart and the head both grow, man will remain in misery and the misery will go on growing. As we become more and more hung up in the head, as we become more and more oblivious of the existence of the heart, we will become more and more miserable. We are creating hell on earth and we will create more and more of it.

Paradise belongs to the heart. But this is what has happened: the heart is completely forgotten; nobody understands that language anymore. We understand logic; we don't understand love. We understand mathematics; we don't understand music. We become more and more accustomed to the ways of the world and nobody seems to have the guts to move into the unknown paths, the unknown labyrinths of love, of the heart. We have become very much attuned to the world of prose, and poetry has simply become nonexistent.

The poet has died, and the poet is the bridge between the scientist and the mystic. The bridge has disappeared. On one hand stands the scientist—very powerful, tremendously powerful, ready to destroy the whole earth, the whole of life—and on the other hand, far and few between stand a few mystics—a Buddha, a Jesus, a Zarathustra, a Kabir. They are utterly powerless in the sense that we understand power, and immensely powerful in a totally different sense—but we don't know that language at all. And the poet has died; that has been the greatest calamity. The poet is disappearing.

And by poet I mean the painter, the sculptor. All that is creative in man is becoming reduced to producing more and more commodities. The creative is losing its grip and the productive is becoming the goal of life.

Instead of creativity we value productivity: we talk about how to produce more. Production can give you things but cannot give you values. Production can make you rich outwardly but it will impoverish you inwardly. Production is not creation. Production is very mediocre and any stupid person can do it; one simply needs to learn the knack of it.

And the poet has died; the poet exists no more. And what exists in the name of poetry is almost prose. What exists in the name of painting is more or less insane. You can see Picasso, Dalí, and others—it is pathological! Picasso is a genius but ill, pathological. His painting is nothing but a catharsis; it helps him—it is a kind of vomiting. When you have something wrong with your stomach the vomiting relieves you. It helped Picasso; if he had been prevented from painting he would have gone mad. Painting was good for him; it saved him from becoming insane; it released his insanity onto the canvas. But what about those who purchase those paintings, who hang them in their bedrooms and look at them? They will start becoming ill at ease.

It is a totally different creativity I am talking about. A Taj Mahal . . . just watch it on a full-moon night, and a great meditation is bound to arise in you. Or the temples of Khajuraho, Konarak, Puri—just meditate on them and you will be surprised that all your sexuality is transformed into love. They are miracles of creativity.

The great cathedrals of Europe—they are the longings of the earth to reach to the sky. Just seeing those great creations, a great song is bound to arise in your heart, or a great silence is bound to descend on you. Man has lost the poetic, the creative urge, or it has been killed. We are too interested in commodities, in gadgets, in making more and more things. Production is concerned with quantity, and creation is concerned with quality.

You will have to bring the heart back. You will have to be aware again of nature. You will have to learn to watch roses, lotuses again.

You will have to make a few contacts with the trees and the rocks and the rivers. You will have to start a dialogue with the stars again.

PRESCRIPTIONS

✒ THE JOY OF LOVING

Whenever you love, you are joyful. Whenever you cannot love, you cannot be joyful. Joy is a function of love, a shadow of love; it follows love.

So become more and more loving, and you will become more and more joyful. Don't be bothered about whether your love is returned or not; that is not the point at all. Joy follows love automatically, whether it is returned or not and whether the other is responsive or not. That is the beauty of love, that its result is intrinsic; its value is intrinsic. It does not depend on the response of the other; it is totally yours. And it makes no difference to whom you are loving—to a dog, to a cat, to a tree, or to a rock.

Just sit by the side of the rock and be loving. Have a little chitchat. Kiss the rock and lie down on it. Feel one with it and suddenly you will feel a shudder of energy, an upsurge of energy—and you will be tremendously joyful. The rock may not have returned anything—or it may have, but that is not the point. You became joyful because you loved. One who loves is joyful.

Once you know this key you can be joyful for twenty-four hours. If you are loving for twenty-four hours, and you are no longer dependent on having objects of love, you become more and more independent—because you can be loving even if nobody is there. You can love the very emptiness surrounding you. Sitting in your room alone, you fill the whole room with your love. You may be in a prison; you can transform it into a temple within a second. The moment you fill it with love it is no longer a prison. And even a temple becomes a prison if there is no love.

➤ OPEN THE PETALS OF THE HEART

Sometimes the heart is there but it is like a bud, not like a flower. But the bud can become a flower. Do one thing: start a breathing process. Do it whenever your stomach is empty, either before taking food or three hours after you have taken food.

Throw all the air out—exhale deeply, pull the stomach in, and throw all the air out. When you feel all the air is out, keep it out as long as you can, for two or three minutes. Three minutes is the best. It will be difficult, but by and by you will be able to do it; you will be completely starved of air and then it will come rushing in. You will feel great joy in its rush, great vitality, and that rushing will help your heart to open.

You need something to penetrate your heart. So whenever you want to do it, you can. Don't do it more than seven times in one session. You can do it three, four, or five times a day or even more; there is no problem. Just remember to do it on an empty stomach so that you can really throw the air out. Then let it remain out as long as possible. And don't be afraid; you will not die, because whenever it becomes impossible to hold it, your control will be gone and the air will rush in. By and by you will be able to keep your breath out for three minutes, and then when it comes rushing in it will open the petals of the heart.

It is one of the most significant devices to open the heart.

⟶ LET YOUR LOVE BE LIKE BREATHING

If you hoard your breath you will die because it will become stale; it will become dead. It will lose that vitality, the quality of life. So is the case with love. It is a kind of breathing, and each moment it renews itself. So whenever one gets stuck in love and stops breathing, life loses all significance. And that's what is happening to people: the mind is so dominant that it even influences the heart and makes even the heart possessive! The heart knows no possessiveness, but the mind contaminates it and poisons it.

So remember that. Be in love with existence and let your love be like breathing. Breathe in, breathe out, but let it be love coming in and going out. By and by, with each breath, you have to create that magic of love. That will be your meditation: when you breathe out, just feel that you are pouring your love into existence; when you breathe in, existence is pouring its love into you.

Soon you will see that the quality of your breath is changing. Then it starts becoming something totally different from what you have ever known before. That's why in India we call it *prana*, life—not just breathing. It is not just oxygen; something else is there—the very essence of life, the divine self. If we invite it, it will come in, lingering, with the breath.

So let this be your meditation, your technique. Sitting silently, breathing, breathe love. You will be thrilled; you will start feeling a kind of inner dance.

➤ BREATH OF THE BELOVED

The experience of breathing has to be more and more profound, scrutinized, observed, watched, and analyzed. See how your breathing changes with your emotions and vice versa, how your emotions change with your breathing. For example, when you are afraid, watch the change in your breathing. Then one day try to change your breathing to the same pattern as when you were afraid. You will be surprised that if you change your breathing to exactly what it was when you were afraid, fear will arise in you—immediately.

Watch your breathing when you are deeply in love with somebody. Holding the hand of your lover, hugging your beloved, watch your breathing. Then, one day, just sitting silently under a tree, watch yourself again breathing in the same way. Make the pattern, fall into the same gestalt again. Breathe in the same way as if you were hugging your beloved, and you will be surprised: the whole existence becomes your beloved! Again there is great love arising in you. They go together.

Watch your breathing, because that loving rhythm of breath is most important: it will transform your whole being.

➤ WHEN TWO BREATHE AS ONE

Watch your loving moments more and more. Be alert. See how your breathing changes. See how your body vibrates. Just hugging your woman or your man, make it an experiment and you will be surprised. One day, just hugging, melting into each other, sit at least for one hour, and you will be surprised: it will be one of the most psychedelic experiences!

For one hour, doing nothing, through just your hugging each other, falling into each other, merging, melting into each other, slowly the breathing will become one. You will breathe as if you are two bodies but one heart. You will breathe together. And when you breathe together—not through any effort of your own but just because you are feeling so much love that the breathing follows—those will be the greatest moments, the most precious; not of this world but of the beyond and of the "far out."

In those moments you will have the first glimpse of meditative energy. In those moments grammar gives up and language expires. In the attempt to say it, language expires, and by its very death points at last to what it cannot say.

⟶ HOLD HANDS CONSCIOUSLY

When you hold the hand of your friend, do it with alertness. See whether your hand is releasing warmth or not. Otherwise you can hold the hand and there is no communication and no transfer of energy. In fact you can hold the hand and the hand can be completely cold and frozen. There is no vibration, no pulsation; energy is not streaming into the friend. Then it is futile. It is an empty gesture, an impotent gesture.

So when you are holding the hand, watch deep inside whether energy is flowing or not, and help to direct the energy; bring the energy there, move the energy there.

In the beginning it will be just an exercise in imagination, but energy follows imagination. You can do it . . . Sometimes just count your pulse and then imagine that the pulse is going higher and faster for a few minutes and then count again, and you will see that it has gone faster. Imagination creates the root; it channels energy.

So when you hold the other's hand, hold it consciously and imagine that the energy is moving there, and that the hand is becoming warmer and welcoming, and you will see a tremendous change happening.

⤙ LOOK WITH EYES OF LOVE

When you look at somebody, look with eyes of love. When you look at people, pour love through the eyes. When you walk, walk throwing love all around. In the beginning it will just be imagination, and within a month you will see it has become a reality. Others will start feeling that you have now a warmer personality, that just to come close to you feels tremendously good—a sense of well-being arises.

Make it your conscious effort—become more aware of love and release more love.

⤙ FALL IN LOVE WITH YOURSELF

Experiment with this a little. . . . Just sit under a tree alone and fall in love with your own self for the first time. Forget the world, just be in love with yourself. The spiritual search is in fact the search for falling in love with oneself. The world is a journey of falling in love with others—spirituality is a journey of falling in love with one's own self.

Spirituality is very selfish: it is a search for oneself, a search for the meaning of oneself. It is to rejoice in yourself; it is to have a taste of yourself. And when this taste starts happening within . . . wait a little, search a little. Feel your uniqueness, delight in your own existence because: "What would I have done had I not been born? How could I have complained, and to whom, if I had not been here?"

You are in this existence! Even this fact, even this much consciousness, this much awareness that "I am," the very possibility of a glimpse into bliss—just rejoice in all this a little.

Let the taste of all this soak into your every pore. Allow yourself to be swept away by the thrill of it. Start dancing if you feel like dancing, start laughing if you feel like laughing, or start singing a song if you feel like singing a song. But remember to remain the center of it all yourself, and let the springs of happiness flow from within yourself, not from outside.

4

GETTING TO KNOW YOU

~

The Search for
Your Original Face

DIAGNOSIS

The word *personality* has to be understood. It comes from the
Latin *persona,* meaning an actor's mask. In ancient Roman drama
the actors used to wear masks; those masks were called *persona—
persona* because the sound was coming from behind the mask.
Sona means sound. The masks were apparent to the audience, and
the sound came from behind them. From that word *persona* has
come the word *personality*.

All personality is false. Good personality, bad personality, the
personality of a sinner and the personality of a saint—all are false.
You can wear a beautiful mask or an ugly mask, it doesn't make
any difference.

The real thing is your essence.

Personality is also a necessary part of growth. It is as if you catch
hold of a fish in the sea and you throw it on the shore; the fish jumps
back into the sea. Now for the first time it will know that it has
always lived in the sea; for the first time it will know "The sea is my
life." Up to now, before it had been caught and thrown on the shore,

it may never have thought of the sea at all; it may have been utterly oblivious of the sea. To know something, first you have to lose it.

To be aware of paradise, first you have to lose it. Unless it is lost *and* regained, you will not understand the beauty of it.

Adam and Eve had to lose the Garden of Eden; that is part of natural growth. Only Adam leaving the beautiful Garden of God can become a Christ one day—he can come back. Adam leaving Eden is just like the fish being caught and thrown on the shore, and Jesus is the fish jumping back into the sea.

Primitive peoples, for example, have something in common with very small children. They are beautiful, spontaneous, natural, but utterly unaware of what they are; they don't have any awareness. They live joyously, but their joy is unconscious. First they have to lose it. They have to become civilized, educated, knowledgeable; they have to become a culture, a civilization, a religion. They have to lose all their spontaneity, they have to forget all about their essence, and then suddenly one day they start missing it. It is bound to happen.

That is happening all over the world, and it is happening in such great measure because this is the first time that humanity has really become civilized.

The more civilized a country is, the more is the feeling of meaninglessness. The backward countries still don't have that feeling—they can't have. To have that feeling of inner emptiness, meaningless, absurdity, one has to become very civilized.

Hence I am all in favor of science, because it helps the fish to be thrown on the shore. And once on the hot shore, in the hot sand, the fish starts feeling thirsty. It had never felt thirsty before. For the first time it misses the ocean around it, the coolness, the life-giving waters. It is dying.

That is the situation of the civilized man, the educated man:

he is dying. Great inquiry is born. One wants to know what should be done, how one can enter into the ocean of life again.

In the third-world countries, for example in India, there is no such feeling of meaninglessness. Even though a few Indian intellectuals write about it, their writing has no depth because it does not correspond to the situation of the Indian mind. A few Indian intellectuals write about meaninglessness, absurdity, almost in the same way as Kierkegaard, Sartre, Jaspers, Heidegger. . . . They had read about these people or they may have visited the West, and they start talking about meaninglessness, nausea, absurdity, but it sounds phony.

I have talked to Indian intellectuals, and they sound very phony because it is not their own feeling; it is borrowed. It is Søren Kierkegaard speaking through them, or it is Friedrich Nietzsche speaking through them; it is not their own voice. They are not really aware of what Kierkegaard is saying; they have not suffered the same anguish. The feeling is alien, foreign; they have learned it like parrots. They talked about it, but their whole life says and shows something else. What they say and what their life shows are diametrically opposite.

It is very, very rare that an Indian intellectual commits suicide— I have not heard of any—but many Western intellectuals have committed suicide. It is very rare to come across an Indian intellectual who goes mad; it is a very common phenomenon in the West—many intellectuals have gone mad. The real intellectuals have almost inevitably gone mad; it is their life experience.

The civilization all around, the overdeveloped personality, has become an imprisonment. Intellectuals are being killed by it. The very weight of civilization is too much and unbearable. They are feeling suffocated; they can't breathe. Even suicide seems to be a liberation, or if they cannot commit suicide, then madness seems to be an escape. At least by becoming mad one forgets all about civilization; one forgets all about the nonsense that goes on in the name of civilization. Madness is an escape from civilization.

But to feel that life is utterly meaningless is to be at a crossroads: either you choose suicide or you choose to be a seeker; either you choose madness or you choose meditation. It is a great turning point.

All personality is false. There is an essence inside which is not false, which you bring with your birth, which has always been there.

Somebody asks Jesus: "Do you know anything about Abraham?" And Jesus answers, "Before Abraham ever was, I am."

Now, what an absurd statement but also one of tremendous significance. Abraham and Jesus—there is a big gap between them; Abraham preceded Jesus by almost three thousand years. And Jesus says, "Before Abraham ever was, I am." He is talking about the essence. He is not talking about Jesus, he is talking about the Christ. He is talking about the eternal. He is not talking about the personal, he is talking about the universal.

The Zen people say that unless you come to know the original face that you had before your father was ever born, you will not become enlightened. What is this original face? Even before your father was born you had it, and you will have it again when you have died and your body has been burned and nothing is left except ashes—then you will have it again.

What is this original face? The essence—call it the soul, the spirit, the self; these are words signifying the same thing. You are born as an essence, but if you are left as an essence without the society creating a personality for you, you will remain animal-like. It has happened to some people.

For example, a child was found somewhere in northern India near the Himalayas, a child of eleven years who had been brought up by wolves, a wolf-child—a human child brought up by wolves. Of course wolves can give the personality only of a wolf; so the child was human, the essence was there, but he had the personality of a wolf.

Many times it has happened. Wolves seem to be capable of bringing up human children; they seem to have certain love, compassion, for human children. These children don't have any of the corruption that human society is bound to give; their beings are not polluted; they are pure essence. They are like the fish in the ocean—they don't know who they are. And it is very difficult once they have been brought up by animals to give them a human personality; it is too hard a job. Almost all the children have died in that effort. They cannot learn human ways; it is too late now. Their mold is cast; they have already become fixed personalities. They have learned how to be wolves. They don't know any morality; they don't know any religion. They are not Hindu, Christian, Muslim. They don't bother about God—they have never heard of him. All that they know is the life of a wolf.

If human personality is a barrier, it is a barrier only if you cling to it. It has to be passed through: it is a ladder, or it is a bridge. One should not make one's house on the bridge, true, but one has to pass over the bridge.

Human personality is partial. In a better society we will give children personalities but also the capacity to get rid of them. That is what is missing right now: we give them personalities, too-tight personalities, so that they become encapsulated, imprisoned, and we never give them a way to get rid of them. It is like giving a child a suit of armor and not giving him any idea of how to unlock the armor, how to throw off the clothes one day when he is growing bigger.

What we are doing with human beings is exactly what was done in China to the feet of women. From childhood, girls' feet were bound so that bones broke and their feet never grew and remained very small. Small feet were loved very much; they were appreciated very much. Only aristocratic families could afford them, because it was almost impossible for the woman to do anything. The woman could not even walk properly; the feet were too small to support the body. The feet were crippled; she had to walk with a support. A poor family could not afford it, so small feet were a symbol of the aristocracy.

We can laugh at it, but we go on doing the same thing. Now in the West women are walking in such absurd shoes, on such high heels! It is okay if you do such a thing in a circus, but such high heels are not for walking. But they are appreciated, because when a woman walks on very high heels she becomes more sexually attractive: her buttocks stand out more prominently. And because walking is difficult, her buttocks move more than they would do ordinarily. But this is accepted, this is okay. Other societies will laugh at it!

All over the world women are wearing bras, and they think that is very conventional and traditional. In fact the bra makes the woman look more sexual; it is just to give her body a shape that she does not have. It is to help her so that the breasts can stand out and can look very young, not sagging. And women in "civilized" societies, societies that insist that women should wear bras, think they are being very religious and orthodox. They are simply fooling themselves and nobody else: the bra is a sexual device. There exist primitive societies that have strange customs. Lips are made bigger and thicker. From childhood, weights are hung from the lips so that they become very thick, big. That is a symbol of a very sexual woman—thicker and bigger lips can of course give a better kiss! In some primitive societies the men used to wear a sheath on the genital organs to make them look bigger—the same thinking behind women wearing bras. Now we laugh at such foolish people, but it is the same story! Even the younger people all over the world are wearing very tight pants—that is just to show their genitals. But once a thing is accepted, nobody takes any note of it.

Civilization should not become a tight enclosure. It is absolutely necessary that you could have a personality, but you should have a personality that can be put on and taken off easily—just like loose garments, not made of steel. Just cotton will do, so that you can take them off and put them on; you need not continuously wear them.

That's what I call a person of understanding: one who lives in his essence, but as far as the society is concerned, he moves with a personality. He uses the personality; he is the master of his own being.

The society needs a certain personality. If you bring your essence into the society, you will be creating trouble for yourself and for others. People will not understand your essence; your truth may be too bitter for them; your truth may be too disturbing for them. There is no need! You need not go naked in the society; you can wear clothes.

But one should be able to be naked in one's own house, playing with one's children; sipping tea on a summer morning in the garden, on the lawn, one should be able to be naked. There is no need to go to your office naked—there is no need! Clothes are perfectly good; there is no necessity to expose yourself to each and every body. That will be exhibitionism; that will be another extreme. One extreme is that people cannot even go to bed without clothes on; another extreme is that there are Jaina monks moving naked in the marketplace, or naked Hindu sadhus. And the strange thing is that these Jainas and these Hindus object to Western women because they leave their arms uncovered, they are not wearing proper clothes.

Now, in a hot country like India people coming from the West find it really difficult to wear too many clothes. It looks so absurd to the Western seeker who comes to India and sees people with ties and coats. It looks so absurd! It is okay in the West—

it is cold and the tie is protective—but in India it is an effort to commit suicide. In the West it is okay to have your shoes and socks on, but in India? But people are imitative. They are moving the whole day with shoes and socks on, in a hot country like India. The Western dress in India is not relevant—tight pants and coat and tie and hat—it simply makes you look ridiculous. India needs loose garments. But there is no need to go to the other extreme, so that you start running naked, bicycling naked into the marketplace. It will unnecessarily create trouble for you and for others.

One should be natural, and by being natural I mean one should be capable of putting on the personality, when needed, in society. It functions like a lubricant; it helps, because there are thousands of people. Lubricants are needed; otherwise people will be constantly in conflict, clashing against each other. Lubricants help; they keep your life smooth.

Personality is good when you are communicating with others, but personality is a barrier when you start communing with yourself. Personality is good when you are relating with human beings; personality is a barrier when you start relating with existence itself.

PRESCRIPTIONS

⇀ THE INNER LIGHT

Each child in its mother's womb remains full of light, that is an inner light, an inner glow. But as the child is born and he opens his eyes and sees the world and the colors and the light and the people, slowly the gestalt changes. He forgets to look within; he becomes too interested in the outside world. He becomes so engrossed with it that slowly, slowly, he forgets to look within; he becomes oblivious of it.

In meditation one has to reconnect oneself with that inner source of light. One has to forget the whole world and go in, turn in, and tune in, as if the world has disappeared, as if it doesn't exist.

For at least one hour every day one has to forget the world absolutely and just be oneself. Then, slowly, that old experience is revived. And this time, when you come to know it, it is tremendous because now you have seen the world and all its variety; you have seen all the noises. Now to see the inner silence and the purity of light is a totally different experience. And it is so nourishing, so vitalizing; it is the source of nectar.

So this can be your meditation every night, or in the early morning, or whenever you can find time. When it is easier to forget the world—either late in the night when the traffic has stopped and people have gone to sleep and the whole world has disappeared of its own accord—then it is easier to slip out. Or early in the morning when people are still fast asleep. But once you have started seeing the inner light, then it can be seen any-time. In the marketplace, in the middle of the day, you can close your eyes and you can see it. And even to see it for a single moment is tremendously relaxing.

But start in the night: for one hour just sit silently looking in, watching, and waiting for the light to explode. One day it explodes. You are not to create it; you are only to rediscover it.

⬝ MAKE ROOM FOR JOY

To know oneself is very elementary. It is not difficult; it can't be difficult; you have just to unlearn some things. You need not learn anything to know who you are; you have only to *unlearn* a few things.

First, you have to unlearn being concerned with things.

Second, you have to unlearn being concerned with thoughts.

The third thing happens of its own accord—witnessing.

The key is, one, you start watching things. Sitting silently, look at a tree and just be watchful. Don't think about it. Don't say, "What kind of tree is this?" Don't say whether it is beautiful or ugly. Don't say it is "green" or "dry." Don't make any thoughts ripple around it; just go on looking at the tree.

You can do it anywhere, watching anything. Just remember one thing: when the thought comes, put it aside. Shove it aside; again go on looking at the thing.

In the beginning it will be difficult, but after a period, there will be intervals where there will be no thought. You will find great joy arising out of that simple experience. Nothing has happened; it is just that thoughts are not there. The tree is there, you are there, and between the two there is space. The space is not cluttered with thoughts. Suddenly there is great joy for no visible reason, for no reason at all. You have learned the first secret.

This then has to be used in a subtler way. Things are gross; that's why I say start with a thing. You can sit in your room, you can go on looking at a photograph—the only thing to remember is not to *think* about it. Just look without thinking. Slowly, slowly, it happens. Look at the table without thinking and by and by the table is there, you are there, and there is no thought between you two. And suddenly—joy.

Joy is a function of thoughtlessness. Joy is already there; it is repressed behind so many thoughts. When thoughts are not there, it surfaces.

Start with the gross. Then, when you have become attuned

and you have started to feel moments when thoughts disappear and only things are there, start doing the second thing.

Now close your eyes and look at any thought that comes by—without thinking about the thought. Some face arises on the screen of your mind or a cloud moves, or anything—just look at it without thinking.

This will be a little harder than the first because things are grosser; thoughts are very subtle. But if the first has happened, the second will happen; only time will be needed. Go on looking at the thought. After a while. . . . It can happen within weeks, it can happen within months, or it can take years—it depends on how intently, how wholeheartedly, you are doing it. Then one day, suddenly, the thought is not there. You are alone. Great joy will arise—a thousandfold greater than the first joy that happened when the tree was there and the thought had disappeared. A thousandfold! It will be so immense that you will be flooded with joy.

This is the second step. When this has started happening, then do the third thing—watch the watcher. Now there is no object. Things have been dropped; thoughts have been dropped; now you are alone. Now simply be watchful of this watcher, be a witness to this witnessing.

In the beginning it will, again, be difficult, because we know only how to watch *something*—a thing or a thought. Even a thought is at least something to watch. Now there is nothing; it is absolute emptiness. Only the watcher is left. You have to turn upon yourself.

This is the most secret key. You just go on being there alone. Rest in this aloneness, and a moment comes when this happens. It is bound to happen. If the first two things have happened, the third is bound to happen; you need not worry about it.

When this happens, then for the first time you know what

joy is. It is not something happening to you, so it cannot be taken away. It is you in your authentic being; it is your very being. Now it cannot be taken away. Now there is no way to lose it. You have come home.

So you have to unlearn things, thoughts. First watch the gross, then watch the subtle, and then watch the beyond that is beyond the gross and the subtle.

➤ ARE YOU STILL HERE?

The Zen master Obaku used to ask, first thing every morning, "Obaku, are you still here?"

His disciples would say, "If outsiders hear you, they will think you are mad! Why do you do it?"

He would say, "Because in the night I forget completely. . . . A silent mind with no dreams and no thoughts. . . . When I wake up I have to remind myself again that Obaku is still here. Who can I ask? I can ask only myself, 'Obaku are you still here?'"

And he himself would say, "Yes, sir!"

One has to have a deep respect toward oneself. Rather than repeating the names of Rama and Krishna, it is a great discipline for you just to ask yourself, to call your own name and ask, "Are you still here?"—don't bother that anybody else may be listening—and say, "Yes, sir!"

If you can do this much you will be surprised what a great silence follows. When you ask, "Are you still here?" and you yourself reply, "Yes, sir!," then there follows a great silence. It is also a remembrance of your own being—and a respectfulness, a gratitude that one day more is given to you, that again the sun will rise, that again for one day at least you will be able to see the roses blossom.

Nobody deserves it, but life goes on pouring into you out of its abundance.

➤ FIND YOUR OWN SOUND

Start feeling that a sound is arising upward from your throat—a moaning, groaning, or humming sound. Feel ripples of sound arising. If you start feeling like humming or moaning, go into it. Don't be shy and don't hold it in. If it starts making your body sway, then go into swaying. Let sound possess you.

There is great sound just like a reservoir in your being and sometimes it wants to explode. Unless it explodes, you will not feel light. You have to help it. It wants to be born and you have to be possessed by it; that is the only way one can help it.

Our basic being is constituted of sound; that is one of the most ancient insights into human beings.

Unless you participate, your own sound cannot start working. It cannot work just by your listening to it. It has to become active, moving and alive. So start humming and chanting. Every morning, early in the morning, get up at five o'clock before the sunrise and for half an hour just sing, hum, moan, and groan. Those sounds need not be meaningful. Those sounds have to be existential, not meaningful. You should enjoy them, that's all; that is the meaning. You should sway. Let it be praise for the rising sun, and stop only when the sun has risen.

That will keep a certain rhythm in you for the whole day. You will be attuned from the very morning, and you will see that the day has a different quality. You will be more loving, more caring, more compassionate, more friendly; less violent, less angry, less ambitious, and less egoistic.

If you feel like dancing, dance; if you feel like swaying, sway. The whole point is that you are no longer in control; the sound controls you.

➤ WATCH THE GAPS

Start doing a small breathing meditation.

Sit on a pillow so that your buttocks are a little higher than your knees. Then make your spine straight and erect. Wiggle your body first and feel where it comes to be perfectly balanced, and stop there. Start moving in small circles, smaller and smaller and smaller, just to feel the right place, where you should be. When you have come to feel that this is the most erect position for the spine, the most balanced state, and you are in a straight line connected with the center of the earth, then move your chin up a little so your ears are in a straight line with the shoulders.

Close your eyes and start watching your breathing. First, the inhalation: start feeling it is going in from the nostrils. Go down with it to the very bottom. At the bottom there comes a moment when the inhalation is complete: just a small moment, where inhalation has come to a completion and there is a gap. After that gap exhalation starts, but between the inhalation and the exhalation there is a little interval.

That interval is of immense value. That is the equilibrium, the pause. Again come up with the exhalation, go the whole way up. The same moment comes again at the other extreme. Exhalation is complete and the inhalation has to start. Between the two . . . again the gap. Watch that gap.

For one or two minutes just watch a few breaths coming and going. You are not to breathe in any particular way—just natural breathing. You are not to breathe deeply or anything. You are not to change the breathing at all; you have just to watch.

After one or two minutes, when you have watched it coming and going, start counting. Count one on the inhalation. Don't count the exhalation; just the inhalation has to be counted. Go up to ten and then come back; again from one to ten, again one to ten. Sometimes you may forget to watch the breath; then bring yourself back to watching it again. Sometimes you may forget to count or you may go on counting beyond ten—eleven, twelve, and thirteen. . . . Then start again and come back to one.

◦

These two things have to be remembered. Watching—and particularly the gaps, the two gaps—at the top and at the bottom. That experience of the gap is you; that is your innermost core; that is your being. And second, go on counting but not beyond ten and then come back again to one, and only count the inhalation.

These things help awareness. You have to be aware, otherwise you will start counting the exhalation. You have to be aware because you have to count only up to ten. These are just props to help you remain alert. This has to be done for twenty minutes; you can do twenty to thirty minutes once a day.

If you enjoy this meditation, continue it. This is of immense value.

⌁ FEEL LIKE A GOD

The idea of being a god can help you immensely.

Just start living that way. Walk like a god, walk as you

would if you were a god, and you will suddenly see many changes happening in your energy. Sit like a god, talk, and behave like a god. But always remember that you are a god—and so is the other. Look at a tree as if you have created it. You are a god, and so is the tree.

Soon you will see—once this climate is created by you and becomes really rooted—you breathe differently, you love differently, you talk differently, and you relate differently. That climate will change everything around you.

⟶ RELIVING CHILDHOOD

A child needs all kinds of protections, but sooner or later he no longer needs them. But those protections become ingrained and they continue, and sooner or later there is a conflict between the structure and the consciousness.

So there are only two ways to go. One is not to allow the consciousness to grow. Then you are perfectly at ease, but that ease is like death and at a very great cost. The other possibility is to break the structure. And it is easy to break it if you are friendly, understanding, loving, and thankful to the structure, because it has helped you up to now, it has protected you.

The whole of one's life has to become just a story of understanding—no fear, no anger; nothing is needed. They are unnecessary hindrances to understanding.

You have to do two things that will be helpful.

One, every night before you go to sleep, sit in your bed and turn the light off. Become a small child, as small as you can conceive of, as you can remember—maybe three years old, because that seems to be the last memory. Beyond that we have forgotten, almost completely forgotten. Become a three-year-old child. All is darkness and the child is alone. Start crying, sway, and start gibberish—any sounds, any nonsense words. No need to make any sense out of it, because whenever you start making sense, you start controlling and censuring. No need to make any sense—anything goes. Sway, cry, weep, and laugh. Be crazy and let things come.

You will be surprised: many sounds start coming up, surfacing. Soon you will get into it and it becomes a great, passionate meditation. If shouting comes, shout—to nobody at all, unaddressed; just enjoy it for the sheer fun of it for ten to fifteen minutes.

Then go to sleep. With that simplicity and innocence of a child, go to sleep.

This will be one of the most important things to melt the whole structure around your heart and to become a child again. This is for the night.

And two, in the daytime, whenever you find any opportunity, become a child again. If you are on the beach, run like a child or start collecting seashells and colored stones. Or if you are in the garden, become a child again; start running after butterflies. Forget your age—play with the birds or with the animals. And whenever you can find children, mix with them; don't remain adult. That is whenever possible. Just lying on the lawn, feel like a small child under the sun. Whenever it is possible, be nude so you can feel like a child again.

All that is needed is to connect yourself with your childhood again. You have to go back in time in your memories. You have to go to the root because things can only be changed if we catch hold of their roots, otherwise not.

So just do these two things. In the night, this has to become a meditation—every night—and you will be surprised how relaxation comes and how deep your sleep becomes and how restful. In the morning you will not feel that you have been going through some nightmares and are sweaty and have constriction. No, on the contrary: you will feel so utterly relaxed, loose—a small child again, with no rigidity. Then in the daytime, whenever some opportunity arises, don't miss any chance to become a child. In the bathroom, just standing before your mirror, make faces as a child would. Sitting in your tub, splash water just as a child would or have plastic ducks and things to play with. You can find a thousand and one things.

The whole point is to start reliving your childhood.

Something is there, ready to bloom, but the space is not available. The space has to be created.

➤ REMEMBER THE ONE WITHIN

Always remember the one who is inside the body. Walking, sitting, eating, or doing anything, remember the one who is neither walking nor sitting nor eating.

All doing is on the surface, and beyond all doing is the being. So be aware of the non-doer in the doing, of the non-mover in the moving.

➤ MOON DANCE

Dance under the full moon, sing under the full moon, and soon you will find a different being arising in you that is not your personality—it is your essence. The moon will pull it up; you just have to be conscious of it.

Dancing on the full-moon night is one of the greatest meditations. For no purpose, simply dance with the moon, allowing the moon to penetrate you. And when you are in a dance you are vulnerable, more open. If you really become drunk with the dance—the dancer disappears and there is only dance—then the moon penetrates to your very heart, its rays reaching the very core of your being.

You will start finding that each full-moon night becomes a milestone in your life.

5

CLEAR VISION

~

Learning to See
Beyond the Apparent

DIAGNOSIS

Philosophy means thinking about truth, "love of knowledge." In India what we have is a totally different thing. We call it *darshan*. And *darshan* does not mean thinking, it means seeing.

Your truth is not to be thought about; it has to be seen. It is already there. You don't have to go anywhere to find it. You don't have to think about it; you have to stop thinking so that it can surface in your being.

Unoccupied space is needed within you so that the light that is hidden can expand and fill your being. It not only fills your being, it starts radiating from your being. Your whole life becomes a beauty, a beauty that is not of the body but a beauty that radiates from within, the beauty of your consciousness.

PRESCRIPTIONS

⟿ Uncorrupt the Eyes

It is your seeing that determines the world. We don't live in the same world, because our ways of seeing are different. There are as many worlds as there are people, hence the clash. Hence the conflict in love, in friendship—because two ways of seeing can't agree. They overlap or they collide. They try to manipulate each other and they try to dominate each other. Deep down, the fact is that there are two kinds of seeing, and there is a great fight going on about who wins, about whose eye proves to be the correct eye.

When you turn in, there is a third eye. Your two eyes meet at a point deep within you. They will never meet outside— they can't meet there. The farther away you look, the farther away they are; the closer you come, the closer they are. When you close your eyes, they have become one, and that one eye can see the reality as it is. It is seeing without seeing. It is seeing without any medium. It is uncorrupted seeing. All seven colors of the rainbow have fallen into one and become white again.

People are very interested in having beautiful eyes. Rather, they should be interested more in having a beautiful way of looking at things. Rather than having beautiful eyes, have a beautiful vision. *See* beautifully. See the one, the undivided, the eternal—that's what I mean when I say "See beautifully." And it is possible. It is within our grasp; it is just that we have never tried to attain it. We have never looked at the potential at all.

We have never worked out the possibility to its actuality. It has remained like a seed. The third eye has remained like a seed.

Once your energy enters and falls on the third eye, it starts opening. It becomes a lotus, it blooms, and suddenly your whole life pattern is changed. You are a different person. You are no longer the same; you can never be the same again and the world can never be the same. Everything is the same and yet nothing will ever be the same again. You have attained to a single eye.

Meditate more and more with closed eyes; try more and more to see *in*. In the beginning it is difficult. It is very dark there, because we have forgotten even how to look in. It has been neglected, ignored. Slowly, slowly, the rocks of old habits will be broken and you will be able to feel, grasp, grope, and slowly, slowly, you will become adjusted and you will be able to see it.

At first it will be utter darkness. It is just like when you come in from outside where it was hot and sunny and you enter your room and it is dark and you cannot see for a few seconds; then the eyes get adjusted. Slowly, slowly, the room is not so dark. Slowly, slowly, it is full of light.

The same is the case in the inner. For a time everything will become dark, but if you persist—and persistence is meditation—if you are patient—and patience is meditation—if you go on digging and digging, one day you stumble upon the source of your energy. Suddenly darkness disappears and it is all light—and of such a grandeur and such a splendor that one cannot even dream about it.

➤ FILL YOURSELF WITH SUNRISE

For a few people the sun can function as the great awakener; it depends on the type. For a few people the same sun can be very maddening.

You will have to find the right moments, because when the sun has risen too high in the sky, you cannot look at it; it will damage your eyes.

Early in the morning when the sun is just coming up—the baby sun; that's what we call the early-morning sun in India, the soft, baby sun—you can look at it for a few moments and absorb as much energy as possible.

Just drink it, literally drink it. Become open to it and be soaked in its energy. At sunset, when the sun is going down, you can again look at it.

Slowly, slowly, you will be able to close your eyes at any moment and see the sun; then you can meditate inwardly on the sun. But first begin from the outside; it is always good to begin from the outside, from the objective, and then slowly, slowly, move to the subjective.

Once you have become capable of seeing the sun with closed eyes, once you have become capable of the visualization, there is no need to meditate on the outer sun. Then the inner sun will function, because whatever is outside is also inside; there is an immense correspondence between the outer and the inner.

➤

The inner sun has to be provoked and challenged. Once it starts functioning, you will see your life changing of its own accord.

You will see great energy arising in you, and you will see that something inexhaustible is there. You can do as much as you want and still you cannot exhaust it.

Once the inexhaustible source is contacted, life is rich. Then it knows no poverty. Inwardly it is rich. Then nothing matters from the outside; all conditions are almost equal. In success, in failure, in poverty, or in affluence one remains tranquil and undistracted because one knows "My basic energy is within me." One knows "My basic treasure remains unaffected by outer circumstances."

Those outer circumstances are important only because we are not aware of the inner. Once we know the inner, the outer starts withering and its importance simply disappears. Then one can be a beggar and yet an emperor. One can fail in everything as far as the outer world is concerned, yet one has succeeded. And there is no complaint, no scar left; one is utterly happy irrespective of the conditions.

That is something real.

↝ BE WATCHED BY GOD

To imagine that God is observing you is one of the most ancient methods. It changes life altogether. Once this idea gets very deep-rooted—that God is watching you—subtle changes start happening. Suddenly there are a few things you cannot do. They look so absurd if God is watching; they look so foolish if God is watching. And a few things you have never done become easier because God is watching.

↝

It is just a technique to create a new situation in your being. After just seven days you will start realizing that subtle changes have started happening: you are walking differently; there is more elegance, more grace in it because God is watching. You are not alone; the presence of the divine is always following you.

Just think: you are in your bathroom and you suddenly become aware that your child is looking through the keyhole. You immediately change: you are no longer the same person. You are on the street and there is nobody else; it is early morning and you are alone. You are walking a certain way, then suddenly a person appears at the corner and there is an immediate change.

When somebody is observing you, you become more alert and more aware. When somebody is watching, you cannot remain lethargic or unconscious.

This feeling that God is watching becomes part of your being; you will find a great awareness arising in you. So you have to be alert about it. Just sitting silently, close your eyes and feel the divine is watching from everywhere. Just see a new kind of awareness arising in you and becoming a pillar of light.

Eating or talking, remember, and you will see that you are not talking nonsense. You will see that your talk has become more meaningful, more significant, and more poetic, that there is a kind of music in it that has never been there. You are loving a friend and you will find your love has the quality of prayer in it because God is watching. Then everything has to become an offering; it has to be worthy of the divine.

⌁ MOON-GAZING

The full-moon night has a very alchemical impact on the human consciousness.

Next time when the full-moon night is going to come, start at least five days before it comes, sitting in the night, just waiting. Wait one hour every night for five days. Then the full moon will come and that night wait for at least two or three hours. Not that you have to do anything; you are just there, available. If it happens, you are ready; if it doesn't happen, there is nothing to be worried about. If it doesn't happen, don't feel frustrated, because it has nothing to do with your doing. If it happens, don't feel that you have done a great thing; otherwise it will never happen again. If it happens, feel grateful; if it doesn't happen, simply wait again.

Each full-moon night start waiting. Don't bring desire in, because that is a disturbance and poisons the whole thing. It is a door of the beyond. Just start waiting for it . . . waiting but with tremendous patience, with no hurry. Don't try to drag it.

It is beyond human control, but one can manage to invite it in a very indirect way.

Take a bath, sing a song, sit silently in the night—wait for it. Sway with the moon, look at the moon, and feel full with the moon. Feel the moon showering on you; dance a little, sit again, and wait.

Let the full-moon night become your particular night for meditation—it will be helpful.

THE SOURCE OF LIGHT

Meditate on light outwardly and inwardly. Let light become your companion; think of it and contemplate on it.

Just watch; observe a star appearing or disappearing in the sky, the sunrise or the sunset, the moon, or just a candle in the room. Then sometimes just close your eyes and start searching for the inner light.

One day you will stumble upon it, and that day is a day of great discovery; no other discovery is comparable to it. That day you become an immortal.

➤ THIRD EYE MEDITATION

The body should be in such a relaxed state that you can forget it; that's the whole thing. If you can forget the body, that's the right posture. So in any way you find that you can forget it, that's the right posture. Just make yourself comfortable, as comfortable as possible. And drop the old traditional idea that if you are meditating, you have to be somehow uncomfortable. That is foolish, just foolish.

Massage the third eye, the space between the eyebrows, for three minutes. The hollow of the palm should be on the third eye and then rub upward, very slowly, very softly, and very lovingly. There should be the feeling inside you that you are trying to open a window. The third eye is the window, and this rubbing will help. If you feel after three minutes that it has not affected your energy, then start rubbing in a clockwise direction.

There are two types of people. A few people's third eye opens by rubbing upward, and a few people's third eye opens by rubbing downward. More people open with the upward movement, so first try that.

And then you have to actually visualize a small point of light just between the two eyebrows at the third eye center. To have the feel, you can put a *bindi* there, the small ornament that Indian women wear on the third eye. You can put it there so you can feel where it is. Then close the eyes and look at that light spot. Imagine a burning starlike thing, bluish, and look upward so that the eyes turn upward.

In fact that particular point is not important; the whole point is that the eyes should look upward. When the eyes are looking upward, the body falls into a tranquility. That's how it happens when you go into deep sleep. The same position of the eyes helps in meditation. So this is just a device to help the eyes to turn upward.

Turn the eyes upward—and sitting in a chair will be easier than sitting on the floor. Don't cross the legs; just keep both feet flat on the floor.

And never put on an alarm. You can just keep a clock next to you, and when you feel like it you can simply open your eyes, have a look, and close your eyes; then that will not be disturbing at all. But never put on an alarm and never tell anybody to knock on the door after sixty minutes, because that comes as a shock and the whole system feels uneasy.

Wear clothes as loose as possible. To be naked is best; otherwise wear just a long robe with no underwear.

Make it one hour. If you can do it twice, it is better, it is very good. If it is difficult to find that much time, then just once, but do it for one hour: the longer the period the better.

➤ DRIVE YOUR MIND UP THE WALL

Start one thing: every day for one hour sit in front of a wall. Look at the wall with half-closed eyes so you can see just the tip of the nose. Sit very close to the wall so there is nothing else you can see.

Be relaxed, and if some thoughts come, just go on seeing that they are passing between you and the wall. You need not be concerned with whatever they are—fantasies, dreams, any-thing . . . nonsense. Go on feeling that they are just between you and the wall.

By and by, after two weeks, you will become aware of what witnessing is.

⟶ BE AN ANIMAL!

Animals have more energy moving into their third eye because their whole body is horizontal. Man is standing vertically. The energy moves against gravity and it is very difficult for it to go higher. It goes up to the eyes only with great difficulty. For the third eye to open, a tremendous rush is needed. That's why many yoga schools use *shirshasan*—standing on the head—to create a rush of energy.

But I don't like that very much because the rush can be too much. It has to be suggested only in rare cases, otherwise it can destroy many very subtle nerves. And once they are destroyed it is very difficult to reproduce them; they are gone forever. A person can attain to the third eye insight but becomes dull as far as other kinds of intelligence are concerned.

But moving like an animal is very beautiful. Then there is not too much of a rush of energy—neither too much nor too little. It is exactly proportionate. And when you are moving like a dog and panting, panting helps the throat center. The throat center is just near the third eye center; the third eye center is just above the throat center. So once the throat center starts functioning, energy starts moving from the throat center to the third eye center.

Animals live in a totally different world, and the whole rea-son that they live in a totally different world is because of their horizontal spine. Man has become separate from the animal world because of his vertical spine. It is good sometimes to become an animal again. It again gives you a deep contact with the whole past, with the whole heritage. Then you are no longer something apart. You are part of the whole animal kingdom.

It releases much spontaneous energy in you, and you will start being less worried. You will think less; you will be more just like animals. They are just there—not thinking of the past, not thinking of the present, not thinking of the future. They are just there, right now . . . perfectly alert, ready to respond but with no idea.

⟶ GOLDEN MIST

Before going to bed, put the light off and just sit in your bed. Close your eyes, relax your body, and then feel that the whole room is full of golden mist . . . as if golden mist is falling all around. Just visualize it for one minute with closed eyes— golden mist falling. Within a few days you will be able to see the whole room becoming luminous in your vision.

Then inhale and feel that that golden mist is being inhaled deep into your heart. Your heart is just void, empty, and that golden mist goes into it and fills the heart.

Then exhale: again feel that that golden mist is going out and that your heart is again becoming empty, void; there is nothing inside. This golden mist filling the heart, your inner being, and then emptying it—just like inhalation and exhalation. With the inhalation you fill it; with the exhalation you empty it.

This you do for five to seven minutes and then simply go to

sleep. But when you go to sleep, always go to sleep when you are empty, not when you are full of the golden mist. Empty yourself and go to sleep. You will have a very different quality of sleep— more of the void, more of nothingness, and more of non-being. In the morning you will open your eyes feeling as if you have been in a totally different land and as if you have disappeared.

In the morning, before you get out of bed, sit again: for five minutes repeat the process. But when you get out of bed, get out full of golden mist. Going to sleep, go when you are empty; getting out of bed, be full of the mist.

Hold the golden mist inside and get out, and the whole day you will feel a subtle energy flowing in you, a very golden energy. In the night become empty and in the day become full: let the day be a day of fullness and the night a night of emptiness.

The next step is that you simply remain a watcher. The golden mist comes in; you are a watcher. Fill your heart; you are a watcher. Empty your heart; you are a watcher. You are neither: neither day nor night, neither emptiness nor fullness, just a witness.

6

MOOD MANAGEMENT

~

Becoming Master of
Your Emotional World

DIAGNOSIS

Misery has many things to give to you that happiness cannot give. In fact, happiness takes away many things from you. Happiness takes all that you have ever had, all that you have ever been; happiness destroys you! Misery nourishes your ego, and happiness is basically a state of egolessness.

That is the problem, the very crux of the problem. That's why people find it very difficult to be happy. That's why millions of people in the world have decided to live in misery. It gives you a very, very crystallized ego. Miserable, you *are*. Happy, you are not. In misery, crystallization; in happiness you become diffused.

If this is understood, then things become very clear.

Misery makes you special. Happiness is a universal phenomenon; there is nothing special about it. Trees are happy and animals are happy and birds are happy. The whole of existence is happy, except for man. Being miserable, man becomes very special, extraordinary.

Misery makes you capable of attracting people's attention. Whenever you are miserable you are attended to, sympathized with, loved. Everybody starts taking care of you. Who wants to hurt a miserable person? Who is jealous of a miserable person? Who wants to be antagonistic to a miserable person? That would be too mean.

The miserable person is cared for, loved, attended to. There is great investment in misery. If the wife is not miserable, the husband tends simply to forget her. If she is miserable, the husband cannot afford to neglect her. If the husband is miserable, the whole family, the wife, the children, are around him, worried about him; it gives great comfort. One feels one is not alone, one has a family, friends.

When you are ill, depressed, in misery, friends come to visit you, to solace you, to console you. When you are happy, the same friends become jealous of you. When you are really happy, you will find the whole world has turned against you.

Nobody likes a happy person, because the happy person hurts the egos of the others. The others start feeling, "So you have become happy and we are still crawling in darkness, misery, and hell. How dare you be happy when we all are in such misery!"

And of course the world consists of miserable people, and nobody is courageous enough to let the whole world go against him; it is too dangerous, too risky. It is better to cling to misery; it keeps you a part of the crowd. Happy, and you are an individual; miserable, you are part of a crowd—Hindu, Muslim, Christian, Indian, Arabian, Japanese.

Happy? Do you know what happiness is? Is it Hindu, Christian, Muslim? Happiness is simply happiness. One is transported into another world. One is no longer part of the world the human mind has created; one is no longer part of the past, of the ugly history. One is no longer part of time at all. When you are really happy, blissful, time disappears, space disappears.

Albert Einstein has said that in the past scientists used to think that there were two realities—space and time. But he said that these two realities are not two—they are two faces of the same single reality. Hence he coined the word space-time, a single word. Time is nothing else but the fourth dimension of space.

Einstein was not a mystic, otherwise he would have introduced the third reality also—the transcendental, neither space nor time. That, too, is there; I call it the witness. And once these three are there, you have the whole trinity. You have the whole concept of Trimurti, three faces of God. Then you have all the four dimensions. The reality is four-dimensional: three dimensions of space, and the fourth dimension of time.

But there is something else. It cannot be called the fifth dimension, because it is not the fifth, really; it is the whole, the transcendental. When you are blissful you start moving into the transcendental. It is not social; it is not traditional; it has nothing to do with the human mind at all.

Just look into your misery, watch, and you will be able to find what the reasons for it are. And then look into those moments when once in a while you allow yourself the joy of being in joy, and then see what differences are there.

These will be the few things: when you are miserable you are a conformist. Society loves it, people respect you, you have great respectability, you can even become a saint; hence your saints are all miserable. The misery is written large on their faces, in their eyes. Because they are miserable, they are against all joy. They condemn all joy as hedonism; they condemn every possibility of joy as sin. They are miserable, and they would like to see the whole world miserable. In fact only in a miserable world can they be thought to be saints. In a happy world they would have to be hospitalized, mentally treated. They are pathological.

I have seen many saints, and I have been looking into the lives of your past saints. Ninety-nine out of a hundred of them are simply abnormal—neurotic or even psychotic. But they were respected—and they were respected for their misery, remember.

Great saints were doing long fasts, just torturing themselves. But it is not much of an intelligent thing. Just for a few days, the first week, it is difficult; the second week it is very easy; the third week it becomes difficult to eat. The fourth week you have completely forgotten. The body enjoys eating itself and feels less heavy, obviously, with no problems to digest. And the whole energy that is continuously being used in digestion becomes available to the head. You can think more; you can concentrate more; you can forget the body and its needs.

But these things simply created miserable people and a miserable society. Look into your misery and you will find certain fundamental things are there. Misery gives you respect. People feel more friendly toward you, more sympathetic. You will have more friends if you are miserable. This is a very strange world; something is fundamentally wrong with it. It should not be so; the happy person should have more friends. But become happy and people become jealous of you; they are no longer friendly. They feel cheated; you have something that is not available to them. Why are you happy? So we have learned through the ages a subtle mechanism: to repress happiness and to express misery. It has become our second nature.

You have to drop this whole mechanism. You have to learn how to be happy, and you have to learn to respect happy people, and you have to learn to pay more attention to happy people, remember. This is a great service to humanity. Don't sympathize too much with people who are miserable. If somebody is miserable, help, but don't sympathize. Don't give him the idea that misery is something worthwhile. Let him know perfectly well that you are helping him, but "This is not out of respect, this is simply because you are miserable." And you are not doing anything but trying to bring the man out of his misery, because misery is ugly.

Let the person feel that the misery is ugly, that to be miserable is not something virtuous, that "You are not doing a great service to humanity."

Be happy, respect happiness, and help people to understand that happiness is the goal of life—*satchitanand*. The Eastern mystics have said God has three qualities. He is *sat*: he is truth, being. He is *chit*: consciousness, awareness. And, ultimately, the highest peak is *anand*: bliss. Wherever bliss is, God is. Whenever you see a blissful person, respect him, he is holy. And wherever you feel a gathering that is blissful, festive, think of it as a sacred place.

PRESCRIPTIONS

➤ OUTSMART THE MIND'S ROUTINES

Feeling sad? Dance, or go and stand under the shower and see sadness disappearing from your body as the body heat disappears. Feel that with the water showering on you, the sadness is being removed just as perspiration and dust is removed from the body. See what happens.

Try to put the mind in such a situation that it cannot function in the old way.

Anything will do. In fact all the techniques that have been developed through the centuries are nothing but ways of trying to distract the mind from the old patterns.

For example, if you are feeling angry, just take a few deep breaths. Inhale deeply and exhale deeply, just for two minutes, and then see where your anger is. You confuse the mind; it cannot correlate the two. "Since when," the mind starts asking, "did anyone ever breathe deeply with anger? What is going on?"

So do anything but never repeat it; that's the point. Otherwise, if each time you feel sad you take a shower, the mind will get into that habit. After three or four times, the mind learns: "This is okay. You are sad; that's why you are taking a shower." Then it becomes part and parcel of your sadness. No, never repeat it. Just go on puzzling the mind every time. Be innovative, be imaginative.

Your partner says something and you feel angry. You have always wanted to hit him or throw something at him. This time, change: go and hug him! Give him a good kiss and puzzle him also! Your mind will be puzzled and he will be puzzled. Suddenly things are no longer the same. Then you will see that the mind is a mechanism, that how, with the new, it is simply at a loss; it cannot cope with the new.

Open up the window and let in a new breeze.

⟶ CHANGE THE ANGER PATTERN

You can release things a thousand and one times, but if the basic pattern doesn't change, you will accumulate again. There is nothing wrong in releasing energy—it is good, but there is nothing permanent about it.

Eastern methods are totally different from Western ones. They are not cathartic; on the contrary, they bring you up against your pattern. They are not very worried about the pent-up energy. They are concerned about the pattern, the inner mechanisms that create the energy, that repress it and make you angry, sad, depressed, and neurotic. The pattern has to be broken. To release the energy is very simple; to break the pattern is difficult; it is hard work.

Now try to do something to change the pattern.

Every day for fifteen minutes, any time that you feel good,

choose a time and close the door to your room and become angry—but don't release it. Go on forcing it, go almost crazy with anger, but don't release it. No expression . . . not even a pillow to hit. Repress it in every way—do you follow me? It is just the exact opposite of catharsis.

If you feel tension arising in the stomach as if something is going to explode, pull the stomach in; make it as tense as you can. If you feel the shoulders are becoming tense, make them more tense. Let the whole body be as tense as possible, almost as if it is a volcano boiling with no release. That is the point to remember—no release, no expression. Don't scream, otherwise the stomach will be released. Don't hit anything, otherwise the shoulders will be released and relaxed.

For fifteen minutes get heated up, as if one is at one hundred degrees. For fifteen minutes work the tension up to a climax. Set an alarm clock and when the alarm goes off, try the hardest you can.

When the alarm stops, sit silently, close your eyes, and just watch what is happening. Relax the body.

Do this for two weeks. This heating of the system will force your patterns to melt.

⟶ Go Deep into "No"

Try this method each night for sixty minutes. For forty minutes, just become negative, as negative as you can. Close the doors, put pillows around the room, unhook the phone, and tell everybody that you are not to be disturbed for one hour. Put a notice on the door saying that for one hour you should be left totally alone. Make things as dim as possible. Put on some gloomy music and feel dead.

Sit there and feel negative. Repeat "no" as a mantra. Imagine scenes of the past—when you were very, very dull and dead and you wanted to commit suicide and there was no zest to life—and exaggerate them. Create the whole situation around you. Your mind will distract you. It will say, "What are you doing? The night is so beautiful and the moon is full!" Don't listen to the mind. Tell it that it can come back later on but that this time you are devoting completely to negativity. Be religiously negative. Cry, weep, shout, scream, or swear—whatever you feel like doing. But remember one thing: don't become happy. Don't allow any happiness. If you catch yourself, immediately give yourself a slap! Bring yourself back to negativity. Start beating pillows, fighting with them or jumping on them. Be nasty! You will find it very, very difficult to be negative for these forty minutes.

This is one of the basic laws of the mind—that whatever you do consciously, you cannot do, and when you do it consciously you will feel a separation. You are doing it but still you are a witness; you are not lost in it. A distance arises, and that distance is tremendously beautiful. But I am not saying to *create* that distance. That is a by-product—you need not worry about it.

After forty minutes suddenly jump out of the negativity. Throw the pillows away, put on the lights, put on some beautiful music, and have a dance for twenty minutes. Just say, "Yes! Yes! Yes!"—let it be your mantra. Then take a good shower.

It will uproot all the negativity and will give you a new glimpse of saying yes. This will cleanse you completely. Without going deep into "no," nobody can attain to a peak of "yes." You have to become a no-sayer, then yes-saying comes out of that.

✐ UNTETHER THE TIGER

Life is such a vast phenomenon, it is impossible to manage it. And if you really want to manage it, you have to cut it down to the minimum; then you can manage. Otherwise life is wild. It is as wild as the clouds and the rain and the breeze and the trees and the sky.

At night start a meditation. Just feel as if you are not a human being at all. You can choose any animal that you like. If you like cats, a cat is good. If you like dogs, good . . . or be a tiger—male or female—anything you like. Just choose one, but then stick to it. Become that animal. Move on all fours in the room and become that animal.

For fifteen minutes enjoy the fantasy as much as you can. Bark as if you are a dog and do things a dog is expected to do, and *really* do them! Enjoy it and don't control anything. A dog cannot control anything—a dog means absolute freedom—so whatever happens in that moment, do it. In that moment don't bring in the human element of control. Be really doggedly a dog! For fifteen minutes roam around the room, bark, and jump. Continue this for seven days—it will help.

If you are too sophisticated and too civilized, that can cripple you. You need a little more animal energy. Too much civilization is a paralyzing thing. It is good in small doses, but too much of it is very dangerous. One should always remain capable of being an animal. If you can learn to be a little wild, all your problems will disappear. So start from tonight—and enjoy it!

⤙ CRISIS INTERVENTION

Whenever there is something like pressure from the outside—and there will be many times in life—then direct entry into meditation becomes difficult. So before meditation, for a fifteen-minute period you have to do something to cancel the pressure; only then can you enter meditation, otherwise not.

For fifteen minutes, simply sit silently and think that the whole world is a dream—and it is! Think of the whole world as a dream and that there is nothing of any significance in it. That's one thing.

The second thing—remember that sooner or later everything will disappear, including you. You were not always here, you will not always be here. So noting is permanent.

Thirdly, remember that you are just a witness. This is a passing dream, a film.

Remember these three things—that this whole world is a dream and everything is going to pass, even you. Death is approaching and the only reality there is, is the witness, so you are just a witness. Relax the body and then witness for fifteen minutes and then meditate. You will be able to get into it and then there will be no trouble.

But whenever you feel that the meditation has become simple, stop it; otherwise it will become habitual. It has to be used only in specific conditions when it is difficult to enter meditation. If you do it every day, it is good but it will lose the effect and then it will not work. So use it medicinally. When things are going wrong and are rough, then do it so it will clear the way and you will be able to relax.

⌁ The Tai Chi of Misery

Whenever you feel you are becoming miserable, go slowly into it, don't go fast; make slow movements, Tai Chi movements.

If you are feeling sad, then close your eyes and let the film move very slowly. Go slowly, slowly, into it, having an all-round vision, looking, watching what is happening. Go very slowly so that you can see each act separately, each fiber separately. If you are getting angry—go very slowly into it.

For just a few days do slow movements, and slow down in other things also. For example, if you walk, walk more slowly than you have been walking up to now. Eating, eat slowly and chew more. If you usually take twenty minutes, take thirty minutes; slow it down 50 percent. If you open your eyes fast, slow down. Take your shower in double the time that you usually do; slow down everything.

When you slow down everything, automatically your whole mechanism slows down. The mechanism is one—it is the same mechanism you walk with, it is the same mechanism you talk with, it is the same mechanism you become angry with. There are no different mechanisms; it is only one organic mechanism. So if you slow down everything, you will be surprised: your sadness, your misery, your anger, your violence— all are slowed down.

That creates a tremendous experience: your thoughts slow down, your desires slow down, and your old habits all slow down.

For example, if you smoke cigarettes, then your hand moves very slowly . . . goes into the pocket . . . takes the cigarette out . . . puts the cigarette in the mouth . . . takes the matchbox out. You go so slowly that it takes almost half an hour for one cigarette! You will be surprised; you will be able to see how you are doing things.

➤ MOON DIARY

The moon can sometimes affect one very much, so watch it and use it. Keep a record each day for at least two months, and keep it according to the moon. Start from the new moon and keep a record of how you feel on the whole that day; then the next day, the third day, then the fourth and every day to the full moon. As the moon starts waning, go on making a record. You will be able to see the rhythm—that your moods will be moving according to the moon.

Once you know your chart exactly, you can do many things with that chart. You can know beforehand what is going to happen tomorrow and you can be prepared for it. If there is going to be sadness, then enjoy sadness. Then there is no need to fight with it. Rather than fighting, use it, because sadness can also be used.

➤ PANT LIKE A DOG

Whenever you feel your belly is in knots, walk and pant like a dog. Let your tongue hang out. The whole passage will become open. Panting can be very significant. If you pant for half an hour, your anger will flow very beautifully. Your whole body will become involved in it.

Try this in your room sometimes. You can use a mirror and

bark and growl at it! Within three weeks you will feel things going very, very deeply. Once anger is relaxed, gone, you will feel free.

➤ ACCEPT THE NEGATIVE

One has to learn to live with the negative parts of one's being too; only then does one become whole.

We all want to live only with the positive part. When happy, you accept it; when unhappy, you reject it. But you are both. When all things are flowing you feel great; when everything has stopped and become stagnant, then you feel in hell. But both have to be accepted. This is how life is: life consists of hell and heaven together. The division of hell and heaven is a false division. There is no heaven up there and no hell down there; they are both here. One moment you are in heaven and another moment you are in hell.

One has to learn one's negative aspect, too, and one has to relax with it. Then you will be surprised one day that the negative part adds to the taste of life. It is not unnecessary; it gives spice to life. Otherwise life would become dull and monotonous. Just think—you feel happier and happier and happier. . . . What will you do then? Those moments of unhappiness again bring zest, search, and adventure. You regain an appetite.

You have to be with your totality of being. All the aspects of good and bad have to be accepted. There is no way to get rid of anything. Nobody ever gets rid of anything, but one learns slowly, slowly, to accept all. Then there arises a harmony between the dark and the light, and it is beautiful. Because of the contrast, life becomes a harmony.

So try to live these moments, too. Don't make problems.

Don't start thinking, "What should I do so I am no longer rest-less?" When restless, be restless! When unhappy, be unhappy, and don't make much fuss about it—just be unhappy; what else can you do?

It is just like the climate: it is summer and the heat is there, so what can you do? While it is hot, be hot and perspire, and when it is cold, shiver and enjoy it! Slowly, slowly, you will see the interrelationships of the polar opposites. And the day you understand this polarity, is a day of great understanding and revelation.

➤ ON CLOUD NINE

Bliss is a very nebulous thing; it is like a cloud, indefinable and continuously changing. It is neither temporary nor permanent. It is eternal. But it is not dead; it is very, very alive. It is life itself, so it is not static, it is dynamic. It goes on changing. That is the paradox of bliss: it is eternal and yet changing, each moment new and yet always the old. In a way, it has always been; in a way, every moment you will feel ecstatic and excited. Every moment you will be surprised by it. So it is very nebulous and it cannot be categorized as momentary or permanent.

Start feeling this cloud of bliss around you.

Sitting silently, feel a cloud surrounding you. Relax into that cloud, and after a few days you will feel that it has become a reality . . . Because it is there; it is just that you have not felt it yet. It is there. Everybody lives in a cloud of bliss—one has just to recognize it, that's all. We are born with it. It is our aura; it is our very nature, our intrinsic nature. So just sit silently some-times, relaxed, and feel that you are losing yourself in a cloud of bliss that surrounds you, constantly changing and yet remaining with you.

As you start losing yourself you will feel more and more blissful. There will be some rare moments when you are completely lost, when the cloud is, and you are not. Those are the moments of *satori* or *samadhi*. They are the first glimpses, faraway glimpses but yet of the truth.

Once the seed is there, the tree will be coming.

⟶ IMAGINE THAT!

If you have a strong imagination, and if you can use your capacity consciously, it can be an immense help. If you don't use it consciously, it can become a barrier. If one has some capacity, one has to use it; otherwise it becomes like a rock on the path. One has to step over it and transform it into a stepping-stone.

Start doing three things.

The first thing: Imagine yourself as happy as possible. Within a week you will start feeling that you are becoming very happy for no reason at all. That will be proof of your dormant capacity. So the first thing to do in the morning is to imagine yourself tremendously happy. Get out of bed in a very happy mood—radiant, bubbling, and expectant, as if something perfect, of infinite value, is going to open or happen that day. Get out of bed in a very positive and hopeful mood, with the feeling that this day is not going to be an ordinary day—that something exceptional and extraordinary is waiting for you, that something is very close by. Try and remember it again and again for the whole day. Within seven days you will see that your whole pattern, your whole style, your whole vibration, has changed.

The second thing: When you go to sleep in the night, just imagine that you are falling into God's hands . . . as if existence is supporting you, as if you are falling asleep in its lap. Just visualize that and fall asleep. The one thing to continue is that imagining and to let sleep come, so that the imagination enters into sleep and they are overlapping. This is the second thing.

The third thing: Don't imagine any negative thing, because if people who have an imaginative capacity imagine negative things, they start happening. If you think that you are going to become ill, you will become ill. If you think that somebody is coming and he is going to be rude to you, he will be. Your very imagination will create the situation.

First start the morning and night imagination, and remember not to imagine anything negative for the whole day. If the idea comes, immediately change it to a positive thing. Say no to it. Drop it immediately and then throw it away.

⟶ SMILE FROM THE BELLY

Whenever you are sitting and have nothing to do, just relax your lower jaw and open the mouth slightly. Start breathing through the mouth but not deeply. Just let the body breathe so the breathing will be shallow and will become shallower and shallower. When you feel that the breathing has become very shallow and the mouth is open and your jaw is relaxed, your whole body will feel very relaxed.

In that moment, start feeling a smile—not on the face but all over your inner being. You will be able to. It is not a smile that comes on the lips; it is an existential smile that spreads just inside.

Try this tonight and you will know what it is . . . because it cannot be explained. No need to smile with the lips, with the face; it is as if you are smiling from the belly; the belly is smiling. It is a smile, not laughter, so it is very soft, delicate, and fragile, like a small rose opening in the belly, its fragrance spreading all over the body.

Once you have known what this smile is you can remain happy for twenty-four hours. Whenever you feel that you are missing that happiness, just close your eyes and catch hold of that smile again and it will be there. In the daytime, as many times as you want, you can catch hold of it. It is always there.

➤ BREAK DOWN THE GREAT WALL OF CHINA

For the whole of life, many people have been going only so far in everything. If you were angry you went only so far. If you were sad you went only so far. If you were happy you went only so far. There is a subtle line beyond which you have never gone; everything goes there and stops. It has become almost automatic, so that the moment you reach that line you are immediately put off.

Everybody has been taught that way—that you are allowed a certain anger but not more than that because more than that can be dangerous. You are allowed a certain happiness but not more than that because happiness can be maddening. You are allowed sadness only up to a point but not more than that because more than that can be suicidal. You have been trained and there is a China Wall around you and everybody else. You never go beyond it. That is your only space, your only freedom, so when you start becoming happy or joyous, that China Wall comes in the way. So you have to be aware of that.

Start doing one experiment that will help tremendously. It is called the method of exaggeration. It is one of the most ancient Tibetan methods of meditation. If you are feeling sad, close your eyes and exaggerate sadness. Go into it as much as possible; go beyond the limit. If you want to moan and sob and weep, do that. If you feel like rolling on the floor, do it but go beyond the ordinary limit, to where you have never gone before.

Exaggerate it because that limit, that constant boundary that you have lived within, has become so much of a routine that unless you go beyond it you will never be aware. It is part of your habitual mind, so you can become angry but you will not become aware of it unless you go beyond the boundary. Then suddenly it comes into your awareness because something is happening that has never happened before.

So do this with sadness, with anger, with jealousy—with whatever you are feeling at the moment—and particularly with happiness. When you are feeling happy, don't believe in limits. Just go and rush out of the limits: dance, sing, or jog. Don't be a miser.

Once you have learned how to trespass the limit and how to transcend the limit, you will be in a totally different world. Then you will know how much you have been missing your whole life.

You will come against that China Wall many times, but by and by you will start knowing how to get out of it—because it is really not there, it is just a belief.

➤ CREATE A PRIVATE WORLD

Do this method every night. It is in three steps.

For the first seven days, the first step: Lying down on the bed or sitting, put the light off and be in darkness. Just remember any beautiful moment that you have experienced in the past. Any beautiful moment . . . just choose the best. It may be very ordinary, because sometimes extraordinary things happen in very ordinary places.

You are just sitting still, doing nothing, and the rain is falling on the roof. The smell, the sound . . . you are surrounded and something clicks; you are in a sacred moment. Or one day while you are walking along the road, suddenly the sunlight falls on you from behind the trees and click!—something opens. For a moment you are transported into another world.

Once you have chosen it, continue it for seven days. Just close your eyes and relive it. Go into the details. The rain is falling on the roof . . . the *plop plop* of the sound . . . the smell . . . the very texture of the moment. . . . A bird is singing, a dog is barking . . . a plate has fallen—all the sounds. Go into all the details from all sides, multidimensionally, through all the senses. Every night you will find that you are moving into deeper details—recalling things that you may even have missed in the real moment but that your mind has recorded. Whether you miss the moment or not, the mind goes on recording.

You will come to feel subtle nuances that you were not aware that you had experienced. When your consciousness is focused on that moment, the moment will be there again. You will start feeling new things. You will suddenly come to recognize that they were there but you had missed them at that moment. But the mind records it all. It is a very, very reliable servant—tremendously capable.

By the seventh day you will be able to see it so clearly that you will feel that you have never seen any real moment as clearly as this one.

After seven days do the same thing, but add one more thing. On the eighth day, feel the space around you. Feel that the climate is surrounding you from all sides—up to three feet away. Just feel an aura of that moment surrounding you. By the fourteenth day you will almost be able to be in a totally different world, although conscious that beyond that three feet a totally different time and a totally different dimension is present.

Then the third week something more has to be added. Live the moment, be surrounded by it, and now, create imaginary anti-space.

For example, you are feeling very good; for three feet you are surrounded by that goodness, that divinity. Now think of a situation: somebody insults you, but the insult comes only up to the limit. There is a fence and the insult cannot enter you. It comes like an arrow and falls there. Or remember some sad moment: you are hurt, but that hurt comes to the glass wall that is surrounding you and falls there. It never reaches you. You will be able to see by the third week—if the first two weeks have gone right—that everything comes up to that three-foot limit and nothing penetrates you.

Then from the fourth week continue to keep that aura with you. Going to the market or talking to people, continuously have it in the mind.

You will be tremendously thrilled. You will move in the world having your own world, a private world, continuously with you.

That will make you capable of living in the present—

because, in fact, you are continuously bombarded by thousands and thousands of things. And they catch your attention—if you don't have a protective aura around you, you are vulnerable. A dog barks—suddenly the mind has been pulled in that direction. The dog comes into the memory. Now you have many dogs in the memory from the past. Your friend has a dog; now from the dog you go to your friend, then to the friend's sister with whom you had fallen in love. Now the whole nonsense starts. The barking of this dog was in the present but it led you somewhere else into the past. It may lead you into the future; there is no way of saying. Anything can lead to anything; it is very complicated.

So one needs a surrounding, a protective aura. The dog goes on barking but you remain in yourself—settled, calm, quiet, and centered.

Carry that aura for a few days or a few months. When you see that now it is not needed, you can drop it. Once you know how to be herenow, once you have enjoyed the beauty of it, the tremendous bliss of it, you can drop the aura.

⤜ HAPPY FEET

When you laugh, laugh through your whole body—that's the point to be understood. You can laugh only with the lips, you can laugh with the throat; that is not going to be very deep.

So sit on the floor in the middle of the room and feel as if laughter is coming from the very soles of your feet. First close your eyes and then feel that ripples of laughter are coming from your feet. They are very subtle. Then they come to the belly and become more visible; the belly starts shaking and trembling. Then bring it to the heart; then the heart feels so full. Then bring it to the throat and then to the lips. You can laugh with the lips and the throat; you can make noise that sounds like laughter but it will not be and it will not be of much help. It will again be a mechanical act.

When you start laughing, imagine that you are a small child. Visualize yourself as a small child. When small children laugh, they start rolling on the floor. If you feel like it, start rolling. The whole thing is to get totally involved in it. The noise is not as meaningful as the involvement. Once it starts, you will know.

For two to three days you might not be able to feel whether it is happening or not, but it is going to happen. Bring it from the very roots—just as a flower comes to a tree, it travels from the very roots. By and by it comes up. You cannot see it anywhere else; only when it comes and flowers on top can you see it. But it is coming from the roots, from very deep underground. It has traveled along from the depths.

In exactly the same way, laughter should start from the feet and then move upward. Allow the whole body to be shaken by it. Feel the trembling vibration and cooperate with that vibration. Don't remain stiff; relax and cooperate with it. Even if in the beginning you exaggerate it a little, it will be helpful. If you feel that the hand is shaking, help it to shake more so the energy starts rippling, streaming. Then start rolling and laughing.

This is in the night before you go to sleep. Just ten minutes will do and then fall asleep. Again in the morning, the first thing—you can do it in your bed. So the last thing at night and the first thing in the morning. The night laughter will set a trend in your sleep. Your dreams will become more joyous, more uproarious, and they will help your morning laughter; they will create the background. The morning laughter will set the trend for the whole day.

Whatever you do in the morning, first thing—whatever it is—sets the trend for the whole day.

If you become angry the first thing, that becomes a chain. One anger leads to another anger, then another anger leads to another. You feel very vulnerable—any small thing gives you a feeling of being hurt; it feels insulting. One thing leads to another. Laughter is really the best thing to start with, but let it be a total thing. Throughout the whole day, whenever there is an opportunity, don't miss—laugh!

☞ YES MANTRA

I am teaching you to say yes to life, to love, to people. Yes, there are thorns, but there is no need to count them. Ignore them; meditate on the rose. And if your meditation goes deeper into the rose and the rose goes deeper into you, thorns will start becoming smaller than they are. A moment comes when the rose has possessed you totally; there are no longer any thorns in the world.

Start putting your energy into "yes"—make a mantra of "yes." Every night before you go to sleep, repeat "yes . . . yes . . ." and get in tune with it. Sway with it and let it come over all of your being from the toe to the head. Let it penetrate you. Repeat "Yes . . . yes . . . yes. . . ." Let that be your prayer for ten minutes in the night and then go to sleep.

Early in the morning, again for at least three minutes, sit in your bed and do it. The first thing to do is to repeat "yes" and to get into the feel of it.

During the day, whenever you start feeling negative, just stop on the road, anywhere. If you can say loudly "Yes . . .

yes . . . ," good; otherwise, at least you can say silently "Yes . . . yes . . ." For three weeks practice "yes."

⟶ DON'T BE SAD, GET ANGRY!

Anger and sadness are the same. Sadness is passive anger and anger is active sadness. It is difficult for a sad person to be angry. If you can make a sad person angry, his sadness will disappear immediately. It will be very difficult for an angry person to be sad. If you can make him sad, his anger will disappear immediately.

In all our emotions the basic polarity continues—of man and woman, yin and yang, the male and the female. Anger is male and sadness is female. So if you are in tune with sadness, it is difficult to shift to anger, but I would like you to. Bring it out, act it out. Even if it looks like nonsense, then, too—be a buffoon in your own eyes but bring it out!

If you can float between anger and sadness, both become similarly easy. You will have a transcendence and then you will be able to watch. You can stand behind the screen and watch these games and then you can go beyond both. But first you have to be moving easily between these two; otherwise you tend to be sad—and when one is heavy, transcendence is difficult.

Remember, when two energies, opposite energies, are exactly alike, fifty-fifty, then it is very easy to get out of them because they are fighting and canceling each other out and you are not in anybody's grip. Your sadness and your anger are fifty-fifty, equal energies, so they cancel each other. Suddenly you have freedom and you can slip out. But if sadness is 70 percent and anger 30 percent, then it is very difficult. Thirty percent anger in contrast with 70 percent sadness means 40 percent sadness will still be there, and it will not be possible; you will not be capable of easily slipping out. That 40 percent will hang around.

So this is one of the basic laws of inner energies—to always let the opposite polarities come to an equal status and then you are able to slip out of them. It is as if two people are fighting and you can escape. They are so engaged with themselves that you need not worry and you can escape.

Don't bring the mind in. Just make it an exercise. You can make it an everyday exercise; forget about waiting for it to come. Every day you have to be angry—that will be easier. So jump, jog. scream, and bring it out. Once you can bring it for no reason at all, you will be very happy because now you have freedom. Otherwise even anger is dominated by situations; you are not a master of it. If you cannot bring it, how can you drop it?

In the beginning it looks a little awkward, strange or unbelievable, because you have always believed in the theory that it is somebody else whose insult has created the anger. That's not true. Anger has always been there; somebody has just given an excuse for it to come up.

You can give yourself an excuse: Imagine a situation in which you would have been angry and become angry. Talk to the wall and say things, and soon the wall will be talking to you! Just go completely crazy. You have to bring anger and sadness to a similar status, where they are exactly proportionate to each other. They will cancel each other out and you can slip away.

George Gurdjieff used to call this the way of the sly man— to bring inner energies to such a conflict that they are engaged together in canceling each other out, and you have the opportunity to escape.

➤ NOTE THE INTERVALS

The real thing is in the interval, in the pause between two words, two thoughts, two desires, between two emotions or two feelings. Wherever there is a pause—between sleep and waking or between waking and sleep. In the pause between body and soul—in that interval. When love turns into hate—the pause when it is no longer love and it is not yet hate. When the past turns into future, the pause—when it is no longer there and the future has not yet come, that very small moment—that is the present, that is now. It is so small that it can't be called part of time. It is indivisibly small; it cannot be divided. That pause is indivisible and it comes every moment in a thousand and one ways.

Your moods change from one to another and you pass through them. In twenty-four hours we come across these intervals so many times that it is a miracle how we go on missing them. But we never look in the pause; we have learned that trick, not to look in the pause. It is so small that it comes and goes and we never even become aware of it, that it has been there. We become aware of things only when they are no more, when they have become part of the past. Or we remain aware when they are coming and are part of the future, but when they are really there, somehow we manage not to see them.

When you are angry, you don't see it; later on you repent. When it is very imminent, then you feel it and you are disturbed that it is coming again. But when it is there, suddenly you become blind and deaf, unaware, unconscious. The pause is so small that if you are not absolutely alert, you will go on missing it. It is so small; it can be caught only in absolute awareness. When you are totally there, only then will you be able to see. When one thought goes out of existence and another comes into existence, between the two there is an interval of thoughtlessness. That is the real thing.

I am giving you the whole key. Now you have to start working on your being with this key.

Falling asleep, try to see the pause when you are no longer awake and sleep is not yet. There comes a moment, a very subtle moment, but it doesn't stay long. It is just like a puff, a breeze: it is there and it is gone. But if you can catch hold of it you will be surprised: you have stumbled upon the greatest treasure of life.

Passing through it, even unawares, you are benefited. Something, some of the fragrance of it, goes on lingering in your being even if you were not aware. But from this moment become alert. Slowly, slowly, the knack comes.

⌁ TAKE NOTE THRICE

In Buddhism there is a particular method known as "taking notice thrice." If a problem arises—for example, if somebody suddenly feels a sexual urge, or greed, or anger—the person has to note three times that it is there. If anger is there, the disciple has to say inwardly, three times, "Anger . . . anger . . . anger"— just to take complete note of it so that it doesn't miss the consciousness. That's all—then he goes on with whatever he was doing. He doesn't do anything with the anger but simply notes it thrice.

It is tremendously beautiful. The moment you become aware of it and take note of it, it is gone. It cannot get a grip on you because that can happen only when you are unconscious. This noting thrice makes you so aware inside that you are separate from the anger. You can objectify it, because it is *there* and you are *here*. Buddha told his disciples to do this with everything.

Ordinarily, all the cultures and civilizations have been teaching us to repress problems, so that by and by you become unconscious of them—so much so that you forget them, you think that they don't exist.

Just the opposite is the right way. Make them absolutely conscious, and in becoming conscious and focusing on them, they melt.

⟶ THE LAW OF AFFIRMATION

There is a great law called "the law of affirmation." If you can affirm something deeply, totally, and absolutely, it starts becoming real. That's why people are in misery, because of that law—they affirm misery! That's why people are happy—but only a few people, because only a few people are aware of what they are doing to their lives. Once they affirm joy, they become joyous.

Make it a point: stop affirming the negative and start affirming the positive.

Within a few weeks you will be surprised that you have a magical key in your hands.

For example, if you get sad easily, then every night before you go to sleep affirm twenty times silently and deeply to yourself—but loud enough so that you can hear it—that you are going to be joyous, that this is going to happen, this is already on the way. You have lived your last sadness . . . good-bye! Repeat it twenty times and then fall asleep.

In the morning when you first become aware that your sleep is gone, don't open your eyes: repeat it twenty times.

See the change in the day. You will be surprised; a different quality surrounds you. Within seven days' time you will have affirmed something and known the result of it. Then slowly, slowly, drop all negativities. Choose one negativity for one week, then drop it. Choose one positive quality and imbibe it.

It is all a question of our choice. Hell is created by your thoughts, so is heaven. "A man is as he thinketh." And when you have seen this—that thought can create hell and heaven—then the ultimate jump can be taken into no-thought. One can transcend both hell and heaven. And remember, it is easier to transcend heaven than to transcend hell. So first move from the negative to the positive. It looks paradoxical but it is easier to leave something that is beautiful than that which is ugly. The ugly clings.

It is easier to leave richness than to leave poverty. It is easier to leave a friend than to leave an enemy. It is easier to forget a friend than to forget a foe.

Change hell into heaven—Western religions have never gone beyond that, but the East has tried to—then drop heaven, too, because even a positive thought is still a thought.

Start affirming no-thought, thoughtlessness, and then the ultimate happens.

7

SEXUALITY AND RELATING

~

Learning to
Dance with the Other

DIAGNOSIS

We live together and we never know anything of what togetherness is. You can live together for years without knowing what
togetherness is. Look all over the world—people are living
together, nobody lives alone: husbands with wives, wives with husbands, children with parents, parents with friends; everybody is living together. Life exists in togetherness, but do you know what
togetherness is? Living with a wife for forty years, you may not
have lived with her for a single moment. Even while making love
to her you may have been thinking of other things. Then you were
not there, the lovemaking was just mechanical.

I have heard that once Mulla Nasruddin went to a film with his
wife. They had been married for at least twenty years. The film was
one of those torrid foreign films! As they were leaving the cinema
his wife said, "Nasruddin, you never love me like those actors were
doing in the film. Why?" Nasruddin said, "Are you crazy? Do you
know how much they are paid for doing such things?"

. . .

People go on living with each other without any love because you love only when it pays. And how can you love if you love only when it pays? Then love has also become a commodity in the market: then it is not a relationship, it is not a togetherness, it is not a celebration. You are not happy being with the other; at the most you just tolerate the other.

Mulla Nasruddin's wife was on her deathbed and the doctor said, "Nasruddin, I must be frank with you; in such moments it is better to be truthful. Your wife cannot be saved. The disease has gone beyond us, and you must prepare yourself. Don't allow yourself to suffer, accept it, it is your fate. Your wife is going to die."

Nasruddin said, "Don't worry. If I could suffer with her for so many years, I can suffer for a few hours more!"

At the most, we tolerate. And whenever you think in terms of toleration, you are suffering; your togetherness is suffering. That is why Jean-Paul Sartre says the other is hell . . . because with the other you simply suffer, the other becomes the bondage, the other becomes the domination. The other starts creating trouble and your freedom is lost, your happiness is lost. Then it becomes a routine, something to be tolerated. If you are tolerating the other, how can you know the beauty of togetherness? Really, it has never happened.

Marriage almost always never happens, because marriage means the celebration of togetherness. It is not a license. No registry office can give you marriage; no priest can give it to you as a gift. It is a tremendous revolution in the being, it is a great trans-

111

formation in your very style of life, and it can happen only when you celebrate togetherness, when the other is no longer felt as the other, when you no longer feel yourself as I. When the two are not really two, a bridge has happened; they have become one in a certain sense. Physically they remain two, but as far as the innermost being is concerned, they have become one. They may be two poles of one existence, but they are not two. A bridge exists. That bridge gives you glimpses of togetherness. It is one of the rarest things to come across a marriage. People live together because they cannot live alone. Remember this: because they cannot live alone, that is why they live together. To live alone is uncomfortable, to live alone is uneconomical, to live alone is difficult—that is why they live together. The reasons are negative.

A man was going to get married and somebody asked him, "You have always been against marriage. So why have you suddenly changed your mind?"

The man answered "Winter is coming on and people say that it is going to be very cold. Central heating is beyond me and a wife is cheaper!"

This is the logic. You live with someone because it is comfortable, convenient, economical, cheaper. To live alone is really difficult: a wife is so many things—the housekeeper, the cook, the servant, the nurse—so many things. She is the cheapest labor in the world, doing so many things without being paid at all. It is an exploitation.

Marriage exists as an institution of exploitation; it is not togetherness. That is why no happiness comes out of it as a flowering. It cannot. Out of the roots of exploitation how can ecstasy be born?

There are your so-called saints who keep saying that you are miserable because you live in a family, because you live in the world. They say, "Leave everything, renounce!" And their logic appears to be right—not because it *is* right, but because you have missed togetherness. Otherwise, all those saints would seem absolutely wrong. One who has known togetherness has known the divine; one who is really married has known the divine, because love is the greatest door.

But togetherness is not there and you live together without knowing what togetherness is; you live that way for seventy, eighty years without knowing what life is. You drift without any roots in life. You just move from one moment to another without tasting what life gives you. And it is not given to you at birth. It is not hereditary to know life. Life comes through birth, but the wisdom, the experience, the ecstasy, has to be learned. Hence the significance of meditation. You have to earn it, you have to grow toward it, you have to attain a certain maturity; only then will you be able to know it. Life can open to you only in a certain moment of maturity. But people live and die childishly. They never really grow; they never attain to maturity.

What is maturity? Just becoming sexually mature does not mean you are mature. Ask the psychologists: they say that the average adult mental age remains near about thirteen or fourteen. Your physical body goes on growing but your mind stops at about the age of thirteen. It is no wonder you behave so foolishly, why your life becomes a continuous foolishness! A mind that has not grown up is bound to do something wrong every moment.

And the immature mind always throws responsibility onto the

other. You feel unhappy and think that it is because everybody else is creating hell for you. "The other is hell." I say this assertion of Sartre is very immature. If you are mature, the other can also become heaven. The other is whatever you are because the other is just a mirror; he reflects you.

When I say maturity, I mean an inner integrity. And this inner integrity comes only when you stop making others responsible, when you stop saying that the other is creating your suffering, when you start realizing that you are the creator of your suffering. This is the first step toward maturity: I am responsible. Whatever is happening, it is my doing.

You feel sad. Is this your doing? You will feel very much disturbed, but if you can remain with this feeling, sooner or later you will be able to stop doing many things. This is what the theory of karma is all about. You are responsible. Don't say society is responsible; don't say that parents are responsible; don't say the economic conditions are responsible; don't throw the responsibility onto anybody. You are responsible. In the beginning, this will look like a burden because now you cannot throw the responsibility on anyone else. But take it . . .

Someone asked Mulla Nasruddin, "Why do you look so sad?"

He said, "My wife has insisted that I stop gambling, smoking, drinking, playing cards. I have stopped all of them."

So the man said, "Your wife must be very happy now."

Nasruddin said, "That is the problem. Now she cannot find anything to complain about, so she is very unhappy. She starts talking, but she cannot find anything to complain about. Now she cannot make me responsible for anything and I have never seen her so unhappy. I thought that when I gave up all these things she would cheer up, but she has become more unhappy than ever."

· · ·

If you go on throwing responsibility onto others and they all do whatever you tell them to do, you will end up committing suicide. Eventually there will be nowhere left to throw your responsibilities. So it is good to have a few faults; it helps others to be happy. If there is a really perfect husband, the wife will leave him. How can you dominate a perfect man? So even if you don't want to, go on doing something wrong so the wife can dominate you and feel happy!

Where there is a perfect husband there is bound to be divorce. Find a perfect man and you will all be against him, because you cannot condemn, you cannot say anything wrong about him. Our minds love to throw responsibility onto somebody else. Our minds want to complain. It makes us feel good, because then we are not responsible, we are unburdened. But this unburdening is very costly. You are not really unburdened; you are getting more and more burdened. Only you are not alert. People have lived for seventy years, and for many, many lives, without knowing what life is. They were not mature; they were not integrated; they were not centered. They lived on the periphery.

If your periphery meets the other's periphery a clash happens, and if you go on being concerned that the other person is wrong, you remain on the periphery. Once you realize, "I am responsible for my being; whatever has happened, I am the cause, I have done it," suddenly your consciousness shifts from the periphery to the center. Now you become, for the first time, the center of your world.

Now much can be done . . . because whatever you don't like, you can drop; whatever you like, you can adopt; whatever you feel is true, you can follow; and whatever you feel is untrue, you need not follow, because you are now centered and rooted in yourself.

PRESCRIPTIONS

↙ OPENING AND CLOSING

If you remain closed you remain dead. It is as if when the whole sky was available you were just looking through the keyhole. Of course you can see a little sky from the keyhole, and sometimes a ray of sun passes by. Sometimes you can see a flickering star. But this is unnecessarily hard, and you remain poor unnecessarily.

Come out of it—and you *can* come out of it. Just try one small experiment.

Every night before you go to sleep, just stand in the middle of the room and look at the wall. Concentrate on the wall: not the door, the wall. Think of yourself as just a wall with no door in you, completely closed. Nobody can enter you and you cannot get out—you are imprisoned. Almost become a wall, psychologically. Let your whole energy become a wall, a China Wall.

For ten minutes be a wall and become tense, as tense as you can. Drop all openings and become absolutely closed, what Leibniz calls a "monad," a windowless atom, completely closed within yourself. You will start perspiring; you will start trembling; anxiety will arise. You will feel as if you are dying, as if you are entering your grave. Don't be worried; enter it. Bring it to a climax—this tension, this contraction, and this shrinking.

Then turn, look at the door—keep the door open—and become a door. Start feeling that you are becoming a door; you are no longer a wall. Anybody can come into you; there is no need even to knock. And they can go out; there is no barrier. Relax. Relax the whole body and the whole feeling. Expand. Remain standing there but expand. Feel that you are filling the whole room. Feel that your energy is streaming out of the door into the garden. Just let the energy go out and feel that the outer world is entering you.

For ten minutes become a wall, and for twenty minutes become a door. Then go to sleep. Continue this for at least three months. After the third week you will start feeling so open . . . but continue it.

I am giving you both, the wall and the door, so you can feel the contrast more easily.

Once you can understand your own energy—that it becomes a wall and it becomes a door—then you will become aware of a very beautiful dimension. Then you can feel others' energies. You pass a man on the street and you can feel whether this man is a wall or a door. Now you have an inner understanding about it. Then if you want to relate with this man, don't relate when you feel he is a wall because then nothing will succeed. Only relate when you feel that he is a door.

Many times this can become such a deep experience in relationships that you cannot imagine it. Approach a person when he is a door, and the same person will be totally different. Approach your child when he is a door—then he will listen, then he is ready to absorb what you say. Otherwise you go on shouting and he is deaf; he is a wall. Talk to your beloved when she is a door. Make love to your lover when he is a door. When he is a wall it is better not to disturb him.

But once you know it as your inner feeling, then you can feel it everywhere.

⌒ COMMUNION

Start one meditation together. Just sit facing each other in the night and hold each other's hand crosswise. For ten minutes look into each other's eyes, and if the body starts moving and swaying, allow it. You can blink your eyes but go on looking into each other's eyes. If the body starts swaying—it will sway—allow it. Don't let go of each other's hands, whatever happens. That should not be forgotten.

After ten minutes, both close your eyes and allow the swaying for ten more minutes. Then stand and sway together, holding hands for ten minutes.

This will mix your energy deeply. So ten minutes sitting looking into each other's eyes as deeply as possible and swaying; then ten minutes with eyes closed and, still sitting, sway. Just feel that the energy is possessing you. Then stand and, with open eyes, sway. It will almost become a dance but go on holding the hands in the same way.

Do this for thirty minutes every night for ten days and if you feel good, you can repeat it in the morning also. You can do it twice, but not more than twice.

⌒ THE OCEANIC OTHER

Go to the sea, there are millions of waves. You never see the sea, you always see the waves, because they are on the surface. But every wave is nothing but a waving of the sea; the sea is waving through all the waves. Remember the ocean and forget the waves—because waves don't really exist, only the ocean exists.

Whenever you have time, sit with your friend—your beloved, your wife, your husband or anybody, a stranger will do—just sit and look into each other's eyes without thinking, and try to penetrate the eyes without thinking. Just look deeper and deeper into each other's eyes. Soon you will become aware that the waves have been crossed and an ocean has opened unto you.

Look into each other's eyes deeply, because eyes are just the doors. And if you don't think, if you just stare into the eyes, soon the waves will disappear and the ocean will be revealed.

Do it first with a human being, because you are closer to that type of wave. Then move to animals—a little more distant. Then move to trees—still more distant waves; then move to the rocks.

If you can look deep down into the eyes, you will feel that the man has disappeared, the person has disappeared. Some oceanic phenomenon is hidden and this person was just the waving of a depth, a wave of something unknown and hidden.

Try this. It will be something worth knowing. Wherever you feel any distinction, know that you are on the surface. All distinctions are on the surface; "many" belongs to the surface.

Look deep and don't be deceived by the surface. Soon you will become aware of an ocean all around. Then you will see that you are also just a wave, your ego is just a wave. Behind that ego, the nameless, the one, is hidden.

⌁ UNBLOCKING SEX ENERGY

Every morning after your sleep, just stand in the middle of the room and start shaking the whole body. Become a shaker! Shake the whole body from the toe to the head and feel that it is almost orgasmic . . . as if it is giving you a sexual orgasm.

Enjoy it, nourish it, and if you start feeling that you would like to make a few sounds, make them, and just enjoy it for ten minutes.

Then rub the whole body with a dry towel and take a shower.

Do this every morning.

⟶ WAIT FOR THE RIGHT MOMENT

Before you move into making love, just sit silently together for fifteen minutes holding each other's hands crosswise. Sit in darkness or in a very dim light and feel each other. Get in tune. The way to do that is to breathe together. When you exhale, the other exhales; when you inhale, the other inhales. Within two to three minutes you can get into it. Breathe as if you are one organism—not two bodies but one. And look into each other's eyes, not with an aggressive look but very softly.

Take time to enjoy each other. Play with each other's bodies. Don't move into lovemaking unless the moment arises by itself. Not that you make love, but suddenly you find yourself making love. Wait for that. If it does not come, there is no need to force it. It is good: go to sleep, no need to make love. Wait for that moment for one or two or three days. It will come one day. And when that moment comes, love will go very deep. It will be a very, very silent, oceanic feeling. But wait for that moment; don't force it.

⟶

Love is something that has to be done like meditation. It is something that has to be cherished and tasted very slowly so that your being is deeply suffused with it and it becomes such an overwhelming experience that you are no longer there. It is not that you are making love, you *are* love. Love becomes a bigger energy around you. It transcends you both; you are both lost in it. But for that you will have to wait.

Wait for the moment and soon you will have the knack of it. Let the energy accumulate and let it happen on its own. By and by you will become aware when the moment arises. You will start seeing the symptoms of it, the prelude, and then there will be no difficulty.

⟁ BE WILD AND WATCHING

Then there is no danger in wildness; then wildness is beautiful. Really, only a wild man can be beautiful. A woman who is not wild cannot be beautiful because the more wild she is, the more alive. Then you are just like a wild tiger or a wild deer running in the forest. The beauty of it! But the issue is not to become unconscious.

So the whole method, the whole process of becoming a witness, is the process of transforming the sex energy. Moving into sex and remaining alert. Whatever is happening, observe it and see through it; don't miss a single point. Whatever is happening in your body, in your mind, and in your inner energy, a new circuit is being created. The body electricity is moving in a new way, in a new circular way; now the body electricity has become one with the partner. Now an inner circle is created—and you can feel it. If you are alert you can feel it. You will feel that you have become a vehicle of a vital energy moving.

Remain alert. Soon you will become aware that the more

the circuit is created, the more your thoughts are dropping; they are dropping like yellow leaves from a tree. Thoughts are dropping and the mind is becoming more and more empty.

Remain alert and soon you will see that you are, but there is no ego. You cannot say "I." Something greater than you has happened to you. You and your partner have both dissolved into that greater energy.

But this merger should not become unconscious; otherwise you miss the point—then it is a beautiful sex act but not transformation. It is beautiful, nothing is wrong in it, but it is not transformation. And if it is unconscious then you will always be moving in a rut. Again and again you will want to have this experience. The experience is beautiful as far as it goes, but it will become a routine. And each time you have it, again more desire is created. The more you have it, the more you desire it, and you move in a vicious circle. You don't grow, you just rotate.

If you remain alert, you will see, first, changes of energy in the body; second, the dropping of the thoughts from the mind; and third, the dropping of the ego from the heart.

These three things have to be observed and watched carefully. And when the third has happened, sex energy has become meditative energy. Now you are no longer in sex. You may be lying with your beloved, bodies together, but you are no longer there—you are transported into a new world.

⟶ Enjoy the Time Apart

Love is a relationship between you and somebody else. Meditation is a relationship between you and you. Love is outgoing; meditation is ingoing.

Love is a sharing—but how can you share if you don't have it in the first place? What will you share? Meditation will give you something that can be shared. Meditation will give you the quality, the energy, that can become love if related to somebody.

Meditation is nothing else but how to relate to yourself. If you cannot relate with yourself, how can you expect that you will be able to relate with somebody else? So the first love is toward oneself. Then the second is possible. People rush into the second love without knowing anything about the first.

If you are missing your beloved, remember her, remember him. Write beautiful letters . . . and don't be worried about whether they are true or untrue! They should be beautiful. Write poems, and give one hour to your beloved every night. From ten o'clock to eleven o'clock, turn off the lights, sit on your bed, and remember the beloved, feel the beloved.

In your visualization touch the other's body, kiss, embrace, and go berserk! The other will never be as beautiful as in your fantasies. Real people are never as beautiful—or very rarely. Sooner or later they start stinking! But fantasy is simply wonderful.

➤ BE A SPENDTHRIFT IN LOVE

When the energy moves upward, sex energy is transformed and changes its quality. Then the need for sex will become less and less, and the need to love will become more and more. Energy going downward becomes sex, and energy going upward becomes love.

But don't wait. Start becoming more and more loving toward people. Just become a spendthrift about love. Just be loving toward friends and even toward strangers. Even to trees and rocks, just be loving.

You are sitting on a rock, and just as one touches one's beloved, you will see that if you touch a rock with deep love, there is a response from the rock. You can almost feel it immediately—that the rock has responded. The rock is no longer a rock. Touch a tree with deep love, and suddenly you will see that it is not one way. It is not that you only are loving to the tree; the tree is responding, resonating.

So just be loving in whatever you do. Even if you are eating food, eat very lovingly; chew the food very lovingly. Taking a shower, receive the water falling on you with deep love and gratitude and in deep respect—because the sacred is everywhere and everything is sacred. Once you start feeling that everything is sacred, you will not feel a thirst for love, because from everywhere it will be fulfilled.

➤ THE FIRST AND LAST TIME

Always remember that whenever you are with a person, this may be the last time. Don't waste it on trivia; don't create small troubles and conflicts that don't matter. When death is coming, nothing else matters. Somebody does something, says something, and you get angry—just think of death. Just think of this man dying, or you dying—of what significance will it be, that he has said this thing? And he may not have meant it that way at all; it may just be your interpretation. Out of a hundred cases, 99 percent are one's own interpretation.

And remember, whenever you are with a person, he or she is not the old person at all, because everything goes on changing. You cannot step twice in the same river and you cannot meet the same person twice. You will go to see your mother and father, brothers, sisters, and friends—but they must have changed. Nothing remains the same. You have changed, you are not going to be the same, and you will not find them the same.

And if these two things are remembered, love flowers between these two.

Always meet a person as if this is the first time that you are meeting.

And always meet a person as if this is the last time you will be meeting.

And this *is* how it is.

Then this small moment of meeting can become a tremendous fulfillment.

⟿ RELEASE THE NEGATIVE

Love is always beautiful in the beginning because you don't bring your destructive energies into it. In the beginning you bring your positive energies into it—both partners pool their energies positively and the thing goes simply fantastically. But then by and by the negative energies will start overflowing; you cannot hold them back forever. And once you have finished with your positive energy . . . which is very small, the negative is very big. The positive is just a small quantity, so within days the honeymoon is over and then comes the negative. Then hell opens its doors and one cannot understand what has happened. Such a beautiful relationship—why is it on the rocks?

If one is alert from the very beginning, it can be saved. So pour your positive energies into it, but remember that sooner or later the negative will start coming in. When the negative starts coming in, you have to release the negative alone.

Go into a room, release the negative; there is no need to throw it on the other person.

If you want to scream and shout and be angry, go into a room, shout, be angry, and beat a pillow. Nobody should be so violent as to throw things on other people. They have not done anything wrong to you, so why should you throw things on them? It is better to throw all that is negative into the dustbin.

If you remain alert you will be surprised to see that it can be done; and once the negative is released, again the positive is overflowing.

The negative can be released together only very late in a relationship—when the relationship has become very established. Then, too, it should be done as a therapeutic measure. When the two partners of a relationship have become very, very alert, very positive, have become consolidated as one being and are able now to tolerate the other's negativity—and not only tolerate but use it—they have to come to an agreement that now they will be negative together also, as a therapeutic measure.

Then, too, my suggestion is to let it be very conscious, not unconscious; let it be very deliberate. Make it a point that every night for one hour you will be negative with each other—let it be a game—rather than being negative anywhere, anytime. People are ordinarily not so alert—for twenty-four hours they are not alert—but for one hour you can both sit together and be negative. And then it will be a game, it will be like a therapeutic exercise. After one hour you are finished with it and you don't carry the hangover, you don't bring it into your relationship.

The first step: The negative should be released alone. The second step: The negative should be released at a particular time with the agreement that you are both going to release the negative. At the third stage only should one become natural, and then there is no need to be afraid. Then you can be negative and positive and both are beautiful—but only at the third stage.

If in the first stage you start feeling that now anger comes no more—you sit in front of the pillow and anger does not come—then the first stage is over. Anger will come for months, but one day you will find that it is no longer flowing; it has become meaningless and you cannot be angry alone. But wait for the other person to feel whether his first stage is over or not. If his is over also, the second stage starts. Then for one or two hours—whether morning or evening, you can decide—you become negative, deliberately. It is a psychodrama; it is very impersonal.

You don't hit hard—you hit, but still you don't hit the person. In fact you are simply throwing out your negativity. You are not accusing the other. You are not saying, "You are bad"; you are simply saying, "I am feeling that you are bad." You are not saying, "You insulted me"; you are saying, "I feel insulted." That is totally different. It is a deliberate game: "I am feeling insulted, so I will throw out my anger. You are closest to me, so please function as an excuse for me" . . . and the same is done by the other.

A moment will come when again you will find that this deliberate negativity does not function anymore. You sit for one hour: nothing comes to you; nothing comes to the partner. Then that second stage is over. Now the third stage—and the third stage is the whole of life. Now you are ready to be negative and positive; you can be spontaneous.

This is how love becomes a marriage.

⌐ FROM LONELINESS TO ALONENESS

People think that when they are lonely they have to be sad. This is just a wrong association, a wrong interpretation, because all that is beautiful has happened always in loneliness; nothing has happened in a crowd. Nothing of the beyond has happened except when one is in absolute solitude, lonely.

But the extrovert mind has created conditioning all around, which has become very ingrained: when you are lonely you feel bad. Move, meet people, because all happiness is with people.

That's not true. The happiness that comes from being with people is very superficial, and the happiness that happens when you are alone is tremendously deep. So delight in it.

Just the very word *lonely* creates a certain sadness in you. Don't call it lonely; call it aloneness. Call it solitude; don't call it isolation. Wrong names can create trouble. Call it a meditative state—it is—and when it happens, enjoy it.

Sing something, dance something, or just sit silently facing the wall and waiting for something to happen. Make it a waiting, and soon you will come to know a different quality.

It is not sadness at all. Once you have tasted from the very depth of aloneness, all relationship is superficial. Even love cannot go as deep as aloneness because even in love the other is present, and the very presence of the other keeps you closer to the circumference, to the periphery. When there is nobody, not even a thought of anybody, and you are really alone, you start sinking and you drown in yourself.

Don't be afraid. In the beginning that drowning will look like death and a gloom will surround you. Sadness will surround you because you have always known happiness with people, in relationships. Just wait a little. Let the sinking go deeper and you will see a silence arising, and a stillness that has a dance to it . . . an unmoving movement inside. Nothing moves and still everything is tremendously speedy—empty, yet full. Paradoxes meet and contradictions dissolve.

Sit silent, relaxed and yet alert, because you are waiting; something is going to descend on you. Whenever you sit, just sit facing the wall. A wall is very beautiful. There is no way to move; anywhere you look, there is the wall. There is nowhere to go. Don't even put a picture there; just have a plain wall. When there is nothing to see, by and by your interest in seeing disappears. By just facing a plain wall, a parallel emptiness and plainness arises inside you. Parallel to the wall, another wall arises—of no-thought.

Remain open and delight. Smile or sometimes hum a tune or sway. Sometimes you can dance but go on facing the wall; let it be your object of meditation.

One has to come to terms with one's loneliness one day or another. Once you face it, loneliness changes its color, its quality. Its taste becomes totally different. It becomes aloneness. Then it is not isolation, it is solitude. Isolation has misery in it; solitude has an expanse of blissfulness.

8

MAKING THE BODY-MIND CONNECTION

~

Exercises for
Health and Wholeness

DIAGNOSIS

Mulla Nasruddin was testifying in court. He noticed that everything he was saying was being taken down by the court reporter. As he went along he began talking faster and still faster. Finally the reporter was frantic to keep up with him. Suddenly the Mulla said, "Good gracious, mister. Don't write so fast. I cannot keep up with you."

I am not following the clock at all. But I have come to understand my body. I have come to feel its needs. I have learned much by listening to it. And if you also listen and become attentive to your body, you will start having a discipline that cannot be called a discipline.

I have not forced it on myself. I have tried all sorts of things in my life. I have been continually experimenting just to feel where my body fits perfectly. Once I used to get up early, at three o'clock in the morning. Then at four o'clock, then at five o'clock. Now I have been getting up at six for many years. By and by I watched what fits with my body. One has to be very sensitive.

Now physiologists say that everybody's body, while sleeping, loses its normal temperature for two hours; the temperature falls by two degrees. It may happen to you between three and five, or two and four, or four and six, but everybody's body falls two degrees in temperature every night. And those two hours are the deepest for sleep. If you get up between those two hours, you will feel disoriented the whole day. You may have slept six, seven hours; that makes no difference. If you get up between those two hours when the temperature is low, then you will feel tired the whole day, sleep, yawning. And you will feel that something is missing. You will be more disturbed; the body will feel unhealthy.

If you get up exactly after those two hours, when those two hours have passed, that is the right moment for you to get up. Then you are perfectly fresh. If you can sleep only two hours, even that will do. Six, seven, eight hours are not needed. If you sleep for only those two hours when the body temperature is two degrees lower, you will feel perfectly happy, at ease. The whole day you will feel a grace, silence, health, wholeness, well-being.

Now, everybody has to watch when those two hours are. Don't follow any discipline from the outside, because that discipline may have been good for the person who created it. . . . Some yogi gets up at three o'clock in the morning—it must be fitting well with him, but then all his followers get up at three o'clock and they feel dull the whole day. And then they think that they are not capable of such an ordinary discipline. Then they feel guilty. They try hard, but they cannot win, and then they think that their master seems to be very exceptional, very great. He's never dull. But it simply suits him.

·　　·　　·

You have to find your own body, its way, what suits it—what's right for you. And once you have found it, you can easily allow it, and it will not be forced because it will be in tune with the body, so there is nothing as if you are imposing it; there is no struggle, no effort. Watch, while eating, what suits you. People go on eating all sorts of things. Then they get disturbed. Then their mind gets affected. Never follow anybody's discipline, because nobody is like you, so nobody can say what is going to suit you. That's why I give you only one discipline and that is of self-awareness, that is of freedom. You listen to your own body. The body has a great wisdom in it. If you listen to it, you will always be right. If you don't listen to it and you go on forcing things on it, you will never be happy; you will be unhappy, ill, ill at ease, and always disturbed and distracted, disoriented.

This has been a long experimentation. I have eaten almost all sorts of things, and then by and by I eliminated all that was not suiting me. Now, whatever suits, I eat only that. My cook is in trouble, because she has to cook almost the same thing every day and she cannot believe how I go on eating and go on enjoying it. Eating is okay—but enjoying it?

If it suits, you can enjoy the same thing again and again. It is not a repetition for you. If it doesn't suit, then there is trouble.

One Thursday night Mulla Nasruddin came home to supper. His wife served him baked beans. He threw his plate of beans against the wall and shouted, "I hate baked beans!"

"Mulla, I can't figure you out," his wife said. "Monday night you liked baked beans, Tuesday night you liked baked beans, Wednesday night you liked baked beans, and now all of a sudden on Thursday night you say you hate baked beans. This is inconsistent!"

Ordinarily you cannot eat the same thing every day. But the reason is not that it is the same thing; the reason is that it doesn't suit you. One day you can tolerate it; another day it becomes too much. And how can you tolerate it every day? If it suits you, then there is no problem; you can live your whole life on it, and every day you can enjoy it because it brings such harmony. It simply fits with you; it is in accord with you.

You go on breathing; it is the same breath. You go on taking a bath; it is the same water. You go on sleeping; it is the same sleep. But it suits you, so everything is okay. Then it is not a repetition at all.

Repetition is your attitude. If you are living perfect harmony with nature, then you don't bother about the yesterday that has gone; you don't carry it in your mind. You don't compare your yesterdays with your today and you don't project your tomorrows. You simply live here and now; you enjoy this moment.

Enjoyment of the moment has nothing to do with new things. Enjoyment of the moment has certainly something to do with harmony. You can go on changing new things every day, but if they don't suit, you will always be running from here to there and never finding any rest.

But whatever I'm doing is not forced; it is spontaneous. That's how by and by I became aware of my body's needs. I always listen to my body. I would never impose my mind on the body. Do likewise and you will have a happier, a more blissful life.

PRESCRIPTIONS

↞ CONNECT WITH THE BODY IN HEALTH

Being in contact with the body means a deep sensitivity. You may not even feel your body—it happens that only when you are ill do you feel your body. There is a headache, then you feel the head; without the headache there is no contact with the head. There is pain in the leg and you become aware of the leg. You become aware only when something goes wrong.

If everything is okay, you remain completely unaware. And really, that is the moment when contact can be made, when everything is okay, because when something goes wrong, contact is made with illness, with something that has gone wrong, and a sense of well-being is no longer there.

You have a head right now; then the headache comes and you make contact. The contact is made not with the head but with the headache! With the head, contact is possible only when there is no headache and the head is filled with well-being.

But we have almost lost that capacity. We don't have any contact when we are okay. So our contact is just an emergency measure. There is a headache: some repair is needed; some medicine is needed. Something has to be done, so you make contact and do something.

Try to make contact with your body when everything is good.

Just lie down on the grass, close the eyes, and feel the sensation that is going on within, the well-being that is bubbling inside. Lie down in a river. The water is touching the body and every cell is being cooled. Feel inside how that coolness enters, cell by cell, and goes deep into the body. The body is a great phenomenon, one of the miracles of nature.

Sit in the sun. Let the sun's rays penetrate the body. Feel the warmth as it moves within, as it goes deeper, as it touches your blood cells and reaches to the very bones. Sun is life, its very source. So with closed eyes just feel what is happening. Remain alert, watch, and enjoy.

By and by you will become aware of a very subtle harmony, a very beautiful music continuously going on inside. Then you have the contact with the body; otherwise you carry a dead body.

So try to be more and more sensitive to your body. Listen to it; it goes on saying many things, and you are so head-oriented that you never listen to it. Whenever there is a conflict between your mind and body, your body is almost always going to be right more often than your mind, because the body is natural and your mind is societal; the body belongs to this vast nature and your mind belongs to your society, your particular society, age, and time. The body has deep roots in existence and the mind is just wavering on the surface. But you always listen to the mind; you never listen to the body. Because of this long habit, contact is lost.

The whole body vibrates around the center of the heart just as the whole solar system moves around the sun. You became alive when the heart started beating and you will die when the heart stops beating.

The heart remains the solar center of your body. Become alert to it. But you can become alert, by and by, only if you become alert to the whole body.

➤ MEDITATION IN MOTION

Let your meditation be more and more of movement.

For example, running can be a beautiful meditation, swimming can be a beautiful meditation, or dancing can be a beautiful meditation. Awareness has to be added to movement. Movement plus awareness: that is the formula for you. Run, but run with perfect awareness; keep alert.

It is natural and easy to keep alert while you are in movement. When you are just sitting silently the natural thing is to fall asleep. When you are lying on your bed it is very difficult to keep alert because the whole situation helps you to fall asleep. But in movement, naturally you cannot fall asleep. You function in a more alert way. The only problem is that the movement can become mechanical. You may be just running mechanically. You may become an expert, a professional runner; then there is no need for alertness. The body goes on running like a mechanism, an automaton; then you miss the point.

Never become an expert in running. Remain an amateur so that alertness can remain. If you feel sometime that running has become automatic, drop it. Try swimming. If *it* becomes automatic, then dance. The point to remember is that the movement is just a situation to create awareness. While it creates awareness it is good; if it stops creating awareness, then it is of no use anymore. Change to another movement where you will have to be alert again. Never allow any activity to become automatic.

⤙ IMAGINE RUNNING

If you can run, there is no need for any other meditation—it is enough!

Any action in which you can be total becomes meditation, and running is so beautiful that you can be totally lost in it. You are in contact with all the elements—the sun, the air, the earth, and the sky. You are in contact with existence. When you are running your breathing naturally goes very deep and it starts massaging the *hara* center, which is in fact the center from where meditative energy is released. It is just below the navel, two inches below the navel. When breathing goes deep it massages that center and makes it alive.

When your blood is pure and is not hampered by poisons and used garbage—it is red and alive, full of joy, and each drop of blood is dancing in you—you are in the right mood to catch meditation. Then there is no need to do it: it happens!

Running against the wind is a perfect situation. It is a dance of the elements.

While running you cannot think: if you are thinking, then you are not running rightly. When you are running totally, thinking stops. You become so earthbound that the head no longer functions. The body is in such an activity that there is no energy left for the head to go on and on; the thinking stops.

In meditation you will again and again come to those moments that come in running, and in running you will come again and again to those moments that come in meditation. By and by both methods will become one. Then there will be no need to do them separately: you can run and meditate; you can meditate and run.

Sometimes try one technique: just lying down on the bed, imagine that you are running. Just imagine the whole scene: the trees and the wind and the sun and the whole beach and the salty air. Imagine everything, visualize it, and make it as colorful as possible.

Remember any morning that you liked the most, when you were running on some beach or in some forest. Let it fill you completely . . . even the smell of the trees, the pine trees, or the smell of the beach. Anything that you liked very much, let it be there as if it is almost real; then start running in your imagination.

You will find that your breathing is changing. Go on running . . . and you can do this for miles. There is no end to it; you can do it for hours. You will be surprised that even doing this on the bed, you will attain those moments again when suddenly the meditation is there.

So if someday you cannot run for some reason—you are ill or the situation does not allow or the city is not worth running in—you can do this and you will attain the same moments.

⬧ Talk Yourself into Relaxing

In relaxation you have simply to relax, unfocused—it is just the contrary of concentration. I will give you one method that you can start doing in the night.

Just before you go to sleep, sit in your chair. Be comfortable; comfort is the most essential part of it. For relaxation one has to be very comfortable, so make yourself comfortable. Whatever posture you want to take in the chair, take it; close your eyes and relax the body. From the toes up to the head, feel inside where you feel the tension. If you feel it at the knee, relax the knee. Just touch the knee and say to the knee, "Please relax." If you feel some tension in the shoulders, just touch the place and say, "Please relax."

Within a week you will be able to communicate with your body. And once you start communicating with your body, things become very easy.

The body need not be forced; it can be persuaded. One need not fight with the body. That's ugly, violent, and aggressive, and any sort of conflict is going to create more and more tension. So you need not be in any conflict—let comfort be the rule. And the body is such a beautiful gift from existence that to fight with it is to deny existence itself. It is a shrine and we are enshrined in it; it is a temple. We exist in it and we have to take every care of it; it is our responsibility.

So for seven days. . . . It will look a little absurd in the beginning because we have never been taught to talk to our own body—and miracles can happen through it. So the first thing is to relax in the chair and have the light dark or dim as you like; the light should not be bright. Tell everybody, "For these twenty minutes there should be no disturbance, no phone call, nothing whatsoever," so it is as if the world is no longer there for those twenty minutes.

Close the doors, and wearing loose clothing so there is no tightness anywhere, relax in the chair and start feeling where the tension is. You will find many spots of tension. Those have to be relaxed first, because if the body is not relaxed, the mind cannot be, either. The body creates the situation for the mind to relax. The body becomes the vehicle of relaxation.

Just go on touching the place. Wherever you feel some tension, touch your own body with deep love and with compassion. The body is your servant and you have not paid anything for it—it is simply a gift. And it is so complicated, so tremendously complex, that science has not yet been able to make anything like it.

But we never think about that; we don't love the body. On the contrary, we feel angry about it. The body has been one of the most ancient scapegoats. You can throw anything into it; the body is dumb and cannot retaliate. It cannot answer; it cannot say that you are wrong. So whatever you say, there is no reaction from the body against it.

So go all over the body and surround it with loving compassion, with deep sympathy and care. This will take at least five minutes, and you will start feeling very, very limp and relaxed, almost sleepy.

Then bring your consciousness to the breathing; relax the breathing. The body is our outermost part, the consciousness the innermost, and the breathing is the bridge that joins them together. So when the body is relaxed, just close your eyes and see your breathing; relax that, too. Have a little talk to the breathing: "Please relax. Be natural." You will see that the moment you say "Please relax," there will be a subtle click.

Ordinarily the breathing has become very unnatural, and we have forgotten how to relax it because we are so continuously tense that it has become almost habitual for the breathing to remain tense. So just tell it to relax two or three times, and then just remain silent.

➤ BE MORE SENSITIVE

Be more sensitive. And you cannot be sensitive in one dimension. Either one is sensitive in all dimensions or one is not sensitive in any. Sensitivity belongs to your total being. So be more sensitive; then every day you will be able to feel what is happening.

For example, you are walking under the sun. Feel the rays on your face; be sensitive. A subtle touch is there. They are hitting you. If you can feel them, then you will also feel the inner light when it hits you; otherwise you will not be able to.

When you are lying in a park, feel the grass. Feel the greenness that surrounds you; feel the difference of moisture; feel the odor that comes from the earth. If you cannot feel it, you will not be able to feel when inner things begin to happen.

Start from the outer, because that is easier. And if you cannot feel the outer, you cannot feel the inner. Be more poetic and less businesslike in life. Sometimes it costs nothing to be sensitive.

You are taking your bath: have you felt the water? You simply take it as a business routine and then you are out. Feel it for a few minutes. Just be under the shower and feel the water: feel it flowing on you. It can become a deep experience, because water is life. You are 90 percent water. And if you cannot feel water falling on you, you will not be able to feel the inner tides of your own water.

Life was born in the sea, and you have some water within your body with a certain quantity of salt. Go on swimming in the sea and feel the water outside. Soon you will know that you are part of the sea and the inner part belongs to the sea. Then you can feel that also. And when the moon is there and the ocean is waving in response to it, your body will also wave in response. It waves, but you cannot feel it. So if you cannot feel such gross things, it will be difficult for you to feel such subtle things as meditation.

How can you feel love? Everyone is suffering. I have seen thousands and thousands of people deeply in pain. The suffering is for love. They want to love and they want to be loved, but the problem is that if you ever love them, they cannot feel it. They will go on asking, "Do you love me?" So what to do? If you say yes, they won't believe it because they cannot feel it. If you say no, they feel hurt.

If you cannot feel the sun's rays, if you cannot feel rain, if you cannot feel grass, if you cannot feel anything that surrounds you—the atmosphere—then you cannot feel deeper things such as love or compassion; it is very difficult. You can feel only anger, violence, and sadness, because they are so crude. Subtle is the path that goes inward—and the more subtle your meditation goes, the more subtle will be the feelings. But then you have to be ready.

So meditation is not just a certain thing that you do for one hour and forget. Really, the whole life has to be meditative. Only then will you begin to feel things. And when I say that the whole life has to be meditative, I do not mean to go and close your eyes for twenty-four hours and sit and meditate—no! Wherever you are you can be sensitive and that sensitivity will pay.

Can you weep? Can you laugh spontaneously? Can you dance spontaneously? Can you love spontaneously? If you cannot, how can you meditate? Can you play? It is difficult! Everything has become difficult. Man has become insensitive.

➛

Bring your sensitivity back again. Reclaim it! Play a little! To be playful is to be religious. Laugh, weep, sing, do something spontaneously with your full heart. Relax your body, relax your breathing, and move as if you are a child again.

Regain feeling—less thought, more feeling. Live more by the heart, less by the head.

Sometimes, live totally in the body; forget about the soul. Live totally in the body—because if you cannot even feel your body, you are not going to feel your soul. Remember this. Come back into the body. We are really hanging around the body; we are not in the body. Everyone is afraid to be in the body. Society has created the fear; it is deep-rooted.

Go back into your body; move again; be like an innocent animal. Look at animals jumping, running. Sometimes run and jump like them; then you will come back to your body. Then you will be able to feel your body, the rays of the sun, the rain, and the wind blowing. Only with this capacity of being aware of all things happening around you will you develop the capacity to feel what is happening within.

➤ For Smokers

Sucking the thumb is better than smoking, and then it will be easier to drop smoking.

This is one of the things to be understood: if you were sucking your thumb and then you stopped that, you have chosen smoking as a substitute. Smoking is not your problem—you cannot do anything with it. However hard you try you will never succeed because it is not, in the first place, a problem; the problem was something else. You have changed the problem. The real problem has been dropped and a false problem has been put there instead. You cannot change it.

My suggestion is to forget about fighting with your smoking and start sucking your thumb. And don't be worried—it is beautiful, it is just beautiful. There is nothing wrong in it because it is not harmful. Start sucking your thumb, and once you start sucking your thumb, smoking will disappear. When smoking disappears we are on the right track. Then for a few months go on sucking the thumb so this long habit of so many years—smoking—drops. For six or nine months suck the thumb, and don't be ashamed of it, because there is nothing wrong with it.

So first drop the smoking and instead start sucking your thumb. Go back, regress. After six or nine months, when smoking has completely disappeared, the thumb sucking is replaced. Then start to drink milk every night, from a bottle that you use for babies . . . every night. Enjoy it like a breast and don't be shy about it. Enjoy it every night regularly for fifteen minutes; it will give you very, very deep sleep. Then go to sleep just lying down with the bottle. In the morning when you open your eyes, again you can find the bottle and suck a little warm milk. In the day also—two or three times . . . not much, just a little milk.

So first the cigarette has to be dropped; then you come to the thumb; then the thumb has to be dropped. Then you come back to the breast—this time artificially—and from there, things will disappear. After just a few days you will see that now there is no need. . . . First you will be drinking four or five or six times a day, then three times, then two times, and then one. One day you will suddenly feel that there is no need . . . but this is how it has to disappear.

⟶

If you fight with smoking, you will never succeed. Millions of people are fighting and they never succeed because they never follow the whole procedure. You have to go about it in a very scientific way. You have to come to the root cause. The root cause is that you missed your mother's breast. You could not get as much as you wanted. That desire is lingering, that desire has not gone, and with that desire something of the unsatisfied child will always remain in you. So it is not really smoking that is the problem: that unsatisfied child will be there.

Once this whole problem is tackled rightly, you will find that for the first time you have become grown-up. Once that child disappears and the desire to suck the mother's breast disappears, you will suddenly feel an upsurge of energy; something caged has been freed. You will become grown-up.

Once you know the root, it can be cut. But without knowing the root you can go on fighting with the shadow, and with shadows you will be defeated; you can never be victorious. So make it a one-year program.

Not only will this disappear, you will be transformed through it. Something very basic in you, which is holding you back, will disappear. Your body will become healthier and your mind will become more sharp and intelligent. In every way you will become more grown-up.

⌐ FOR SMOKERS (2)

I will suggest that you smoke as much as you want to smoke. It is not a sin in the first place. I give you that guarantee—I will be responsible. I take the sin on myself, so if you meet God on Judgment Day you can just tell him that this fellow is responsible. And I will stand there as a witness for you that you are not responsible. So don't be worried about its being a sin. Relax and don't try to drop it with effort. No, that is not going to help.

So this is my suggestion: smoke as much as you want to smoke—just smoke meditatively. If followers of Zen people can drink tea meditatively, why can't you smoke meditatively?

In fact, tea contains the same stimulant as cigarettes; it is the same stimulant, there is not much difference. Smoke meditatively, very religiously. Make it a ceremony. Try it my way.

Make a small corner in your house just for smoking: a small temple devoted, dedicated, to the God of Smoking. First bow down to your cigarette packet. Have a little chitchat, talk to the cigarettes. Inquire, "How are you?" And then very slowly take a cigarette out—very slowly, as slowly as you can, because only if you take it out very slowly will you be aware. Don't do it in a mechanical way, as you always do. Then tap the cigarette on the packet very slowly and for as long as you want. There is no hurry here, either. Then take the lighter; bow down to the lighter. These are great gods, deities! Light is God, so why not the lighter?

Then start smoking very slowly, just like a Buddhist meditation. Don't do it like a *pranayama* yoga breathing, quick and fast and deep, but very slowly. Buddha says: Breathe naturally. So you smoke naturally—very slow, no hurry. If it is a sin, you are in a hurry. If it is a sin, you want to finish it as soon as possible. If it is a sin, you don't want to look at it. You go on reading the newspaper and you go on smoking. Who wants to look at a sin? But it is not a sin, so watch it—watch each of your acts.

Divide your acts into small fragments so you can move very slowly. And you will be surprised: by watching your smoking, slowly smoking will become less and less. And one day suddenly . . . it is gone. You have not made any effort to drop it; it has dropped of its own accord, because by becoming aware of a dead pattern, a routine, a mechanical habit, you have created, you have released, a new energy of consciousness in you. Only that energy can help you; nothing else will ever help.

And it is so not only with smoking; it is so with everything else in life. Don't try too hard to change yourself. That leaves scars. Even if you change, your change will remain superficial and you will find a substitute somewhere; you will *have* to find a substitute, otherwise you will feel empty.

And when something withers away of its own accord because you have become so silently aware of the stupidity of it that no effort is needed, when it simply falls, just like a dead leaf falling from a tree, it leaves no scar behind and it leaves no ego behind.

If you drop something by effort, it creates great ego. You start thinking, "Now I am a very virtuous man because I don't smoke." If you think that smoking is a sin, naturally, obviously, if you drop it you will think you are a very virtuous man.

That's how your virtuous men are. Somebody does not smoke, somebody does not drink, somebody eats only once a day, somebody does not eat in the night, somebody has even stopped drinking water in the night . . . and they are all great saints! These are saintly qualities, great virtues!

We have made religion so silly, it has lost all glory. It has become as stupid as people are. But the whole thing depends on your attitude: if you think something is a sin, then your virtue will be just the opposite of it.

I emphasize it: not smoking is not virtue; smoking is not sin. Awareness is virtue; unawareness is sin. And then the same law is applicable to your whole life.

⌐ EAT HUMMING FOODS

There are two types of food. One is that which you like, which you have a fancy for, or about which you fantasize. There is nothing wrong with that, but you will have to learn a small trick related to it.

There are foods that have a tremendous appeal. The appeal is only because you see that the food is available. You go into a hotel or into a restaurant and you see certain foods . . . the smell coming from the back room, the color and the aroma of the food. You were not thinking about the food, and suddenly you are interested in it. This is not going to help; this is not your real desire. You can eat this thing but it will not satisfy you. You will eat and eat and nothing will come of it; no satisfaction will come of it—and satisfaction is the most important thing. It is dissatisfaction that creates the obsession with food.

Simply meditate every day before you take food. Close your eyes and just feel what your body needs—whatever it is. You have not seen any food and no food is available; you are simply feeling your own being, what your body needs, what you feel like, and what you hanker for.

Dr. Leonard Pearson calls this "humming food"—food that hums to you. Go and eat as much of it as you want but stick to it. The other food he calls "beckoning food": when it becomes available you become interested in it. Then it is a mind thing and it is not your need. If you listen to your humming food, you can eat as much as you want and you will never suffer because it will satisfy you. The body simply desires that which it needs; it never desires anything else. That will be satisfying, and once there is satisfaction, one never eats more.

The problem arises only if you are eating foods that are beckoning foods: you see them available and you become interested and you eat them. They cannot satisfy you because there is no need in the body for them. When they don't satisfy you, you feel unsatisfied. Feeling unsatisfied you eat more, but however much you eat, it is not going to satisfy you because there is no need in the first place.

The first type of desire has to be fulfilled and then the second will disappear.

It will take a few days or even a few weeks for you to come to feel what appeals to you. Eat as much as you want of what appeals to you. Don't bother about what others say. If ice cream appeals to you, eat ice cream. Eat to your satisfaction, to your heart's content, and then suddenly you will see that there is satisfaction. When you feel satisfied, the desire to stuff yourself disappears. It is an unsatisfied state that makes you stuff yourself more and more and still to no purpose. You feel full and still unsatisfied, so the problem arises.

So first start learning something that is natural and which will come . . . because we have only forgotten; it is there in the body.

When you are going to take your breakfast, close your eyes and see what you want, what your desire really is. Don't think about what is available; simply think what your desire is and then go and find that thing and eat it. Eat as much as you want. For a few days just go with it. By and by, you will see that now no food "beckons" you.

The second thing is, when you eat, chew it well. Don't swallow it in a hurry—because if it is oral, you enjoy it in the mouth, so why not chew it more? If you take ten bites of something, you can enjoy one bite and chew it ten times more. It will almost be like taking ten bites if your enjoyment is only of the taste.

So whenever you are eating, chew more, because the enjoyment is just above the throat. Below the throat there is no taste—nothing of the sort—so why be in a hurry? Just chew it more and taste it more. To make this taste more intense, do all that can be done. When you are eating something, first smell it. Enjoy the smell of it, because half the taste consists of smell.

So smell the food, look at the food. There is no hurry, take your time. Make it a meditation. Even if people think you have gone mad, don't be worried. Just look at it from all sides. Touch it with closed eyes; touch it with your cheek. Feel it in every way; smell it again and again. Then take a small bite and chew it, enjoy it; let it be a meditation. A very small quantity of food will be enough and will give you more satisfaction.

⟶ SLEEP WELL

Make a regular time to go to sleep—if you go at eleven every evening, then eleven.

The first thing is to stick to a regular time, then soon the body can get into a rhythm. Don't change the time, otherwise you confuse the body. There is a biological rhythm and the body has lost track of it. So if you decide to go to bed at eleven, then fix it; then whatever happens, you have to go to bed at eleven. You can decide on twelve o'clock—whatever time you fix—but then it has to be regular. That's one thing.

And before going to bed, for half an hour dance vigorously so that the whole body can throw out all its tensions. If you have problems with insomnia, you must be going to bed with all the tensions; those tensions keep you awake. So if you are going to go to sleep at eleven, at ten start dancing. Dance up to ten-thirty.

Then take a hot shower or a hot bath. Relax in the bath for fifteen minutes. Let the whole body relax. First the dance, so all the tensions are thrown out, then a hot shower. A hot bath will be far better than a shower, so you can lie down in the bath for fifteen or twenty minutes, or half an hour, and relax there.

Then eat something—anything hot will be good, not cold. Just hot milk will do, and then go to sleep. And don't read before going to sleep—never.

⟶

This should be the program, a one-hour program: dance, bathe, have something to eat—hot milk is the best—and then go to sleep. Turn off the light and go to sleep. Whether the sleep comes or not, don't be worried. If it is not coming, just silently lie down and watch your breath. You are not to breathe too much; otherwise that will keep you awake. Leave the breath as it is, silent, but you go on simply watching it: it is coming in and going out, coming in and going out . . . It is such a monotonous process that soon you will be fast asleep. Anything monotonous is helpful. And breathing is absolutely monotonous, no change. . . . It goes out and comes in and goes out, comes in . . .

You can even use the words *coming in* and *going out, coming in* and *going out.* Inside, just repeat "Coming in . . . going out . . . coming in . . . going out . . ." That becomes a transcendental meditation, and transcendental meditation is good for sleep, not for awakening!

If sleep doesn't come, don't get up again. Don't go to the fridge and start eating things or reading or doing anything. Whatever happens, just remain in bed, relaxed. Even if no sleep comes, relaxing is almost as valuable as sleep; just a little less valuable, that's all. If sleep gives you 100 percent rest, relaxing in the bed will give you 90 percent. But don't get out, otherwise you disturb the rhythm.

Within a few days you will see that sleep is coming. In the morning also make it a point to get up at exactly the same hour every day.

Even if you have not slept the whole night, it doesn't matter; when the alarm goes off you have to get up. Don't go to sleep again in the day because that is how you can disturb the rhythm. How is your body going to get in rhythm? Don't go to sleep in the day; forget about it. Wait for the night and at eleven you will go to bed again. Let the body starve for sleep. So from eleven to six . . . seven hours is enough.

Even if in the daytime you feel like sleeping, go for a walk, read, sing, or listen to music but don't go to sleep. Resist that temptation. The whole point is to bring the body back to a rhythmic cycle.

⟋ TOSS THE TRASH

Before you go to sleep, start doing gibberish. Thirty minutes' gibberish will do. It will empty you so fast. It takes time in the ordinary way: you go on and on ruminating and the thoughts go on and on and on, and it takes the whole night. It can be done in half an hour!

Gibberish, glossolalia, is the best thing: just sit in your bed, turn the lights off, and start talking in tongues. Allow all sounds; anything that comes, allow. You need not worry about language, you need not worry about grammar, and you need not worry about what you are saying. You need not worry about the meaning; it has nothing to do with meaning. The more meaningless it is, the more helpful.

It simply throws out the rubbish of the mind, throws out the noise. So anything—just start and go on, but be very passionate about it, as if you are talking, as if your whole life is at stake. You are talking nonsense and there is nobody except you, but be passionate, be in a passionate dialogue. Just thirty minutes of it will do, and you will have a good sleep for the whole night.

The mind accumulates noise, and when you want to go to sleep it continues. It has become a habit now: it does not know now how to go off, that's all. The switch that turns it on and off is not working. This will help. This will simply allow it to release this energy and then, empty, you will fall asleep.

That's what happens in dreams and thoughts in the night: the mind is trying to empty itself for the next day; it has to get ready. You have forgotten how to put this process to an end, and the more you try, the more you become awake, so sleep becomes difficult.

So it is not a question of trying to go to sleep—don't try anything. How can you try to let go? It happens. It is not something that you have to do. You can only create a situation in which it can happen easily, that's all. Turn the light off, have a comfortable bed, a good pillow, and be comfortably warm. That's all that you can do. Then for half an hour get into a really passionate monologue, a nonsense monologue.

Sounds will come—utter them—and one sound will lead into another. Soon you will be speaking Chinese and Italian and French and other languages that you don't know. It is really beautiful, because the language that you do know can never help emptying. Because you know it, you won't allow things to have their full expression. You will be afraid of many things: What are you saying? Is it right to say it? Is it moral? You may start feeling guilty that you are saying such wrong things. When you are speaking in sounds, you don't know what you are saying, but your gestures and your passion will do the work.

➤ EXHAUSTION RECOVERY

For seven days do a small experiment. It will settle you and will give you great insight. For seven days sleep as much as you can: eat well and go to sleep again; eat well and go again to sleep. For seven days don't read, don't listen to the radio, don't watch TV, and don't see anybody.

For seven days completely stop everything. For seven days simply relax and just lie down, rest. Those seven days will be a great experience for you. When you come out of it you will be perfectly able to adjust to any kind of society and to any kind of work. In fact, in those seven days you will start hankering for work and activity and a great desire will arise to be out of bed. But for seven days stick to the bed.

9

THE EYE OF THE STORM

~

Staying Cool, Calm,
and Connected

DIAGNOSIS

There are qualities that grow as meditation deepens. For example, you start feeling loving for no reason at all. Not the love that you know, in which you have to fall—not falling in love. But just a quality of lovingness, not only to human beings. As your meditation deepens, your lovingness will start spreading beyond humanity to animals, to trees, even to the rocks, to the mountains.

If you feel that something is left out of your love—that means you are stuck. Your lovingness should spread to the whole existence. As your meditation goes higher, your lower qualities will start dropping. You cannot manage both. You cannot be angry as easily as you have always been. Slowly, slowly, it becomes impossible to be angry. You cannot deceive, cheat, exploit, in any way. You cannot hurt. Your behavior pattern will be changing with your inner consciousness change.

You will not fall into those sad moments that you usually fall into—frustrations, failures, sadness, a feeling of meaninglessness, anxieties, anguish; all these are slowly, slowly, going to become foreigners.

A moment comes when even if you want to be angry, you will find it impossible; you have forgotten the language of anger. Laughter will become easier. Your face, your eyes, will be aglow with some inner light. You will feel that you have become light, as if gravitation does not function as it used to function before. You have lost heaviness, because all these qualities are very heavy— anger, sadness, frustration, cunningness. All these feelings are very heavy. You don't know, but they are making you heavy-hearted and they also make you hard.

As meditation grows, you will feel yourself becoming soft, vulnerable; just as laughter will become easy to you, tears will also become easy to you. But these tears will not be of sadness or sorrow. These tears will be of joy, blissfulness; these tears will be of gratitude, of thankfulness. These tears will say what words cannot; these tears will be your prayers.

And for the first time you will know that tears are not only to express your pain, your misery, your suffering; that's how we have used them. But they have a far greater purpose to fulfill: they are immensely beautiful when they come as an expression of ecstasy.

And you will find, on the whole, expansion—that you are expanding, you are becoming bigger and bigger. Not in the sense of the ego but in the sense that your consciousness is spreading, that it is taking people within its area, that your hands are becoming bigger and hugging faraway people, that distances are falling away, that even faraway stars are close, because your consciousness now has wings.

And these things are so clear and so certain that a question or doubt never arises. If a doubt arises, that means you are stuck; then be more alert, put forth your energy more intensively in meditation. But if these things come without any question . . .

This is a strange world: if you are miserable, if you are suffering, nobody says to you that somebody has brainwashed you, somebody has hypnotized you. But if you are smiling, joyously dancing in the street, singing a song, people will be shocked. They will ask, "What are you doing? Somebody has brainwashed you—are you hypnotized, or have you gone mad?"

In this strange world suffering is accepted as natural. Anguish is accepted as natural. Why? Because whenever you are suffering and whenever you are miserable, you make the other person feel happy that he is not so miserable, he is not so unhappy. You give him a chance to show sympathy to you, and sympathy costs nothing.

But if you are so blissful, so happy, then that man cannot feel himself happier than you; you are putting him down. He feels something is wrong with him. He has to condemn you, otherwise he has to think about himself, which he is afraid to do. Everybody is afraid to think about himself because that means changing, transforming, going through some processes.

It is easy to accept people with sad faces; it is very difficult to accept people with laughter. It should not be so. In a better world, in a world with more conscious people, it should not be so, it should be just the opposite, so that when you are suffering, people will start asking you, "What is the matter? What has gone wrong?" And when you are happy and you are dancing by the side of the road, if somebody passes by he may join you, he may dance with you, or he may at least feel happy seeing you dance. But he will not say you are mad, because dancing is not mad, singing is not mad, joy is not mad; misery is mad. But madness is accepted.

With your meditation developing you have to be aware that you will be creating so many critics around you who will say, "Something is going wrong with you. We have seen you smiling when you were sitting alone. Why were you smiling? This is not sane." To be sad is sane, but to be smiling, that is not sane.

People will find it hard if they insult you and you don't react. You simply say "thank you" and go on your way. This is hard to take because it deeply insults the person's ego. He wanted to drag you down into the gutter and you refused; now he is alone in the gutter. He cannot forgive you.

So if these things start happening, you can be certain you are on the right path. And soon people of understanding, people of experience, will start finding the changes in you. They will start asking you what has happened to you, how it has happened to you. "We would also like it to happen to us." Who wants to be miserable? Who wants to remain continuously in inner torture?

As your meditation deepens, all these things are going to happen: somebody will condemn you, somebody will think you are mad, somebody who has some understanding will ask you, "What has happened to you and how can it happen to me?"

You remain centered, rooted, grounded in your being—whatever happens around you does not matter. You have to become the center of the cyclone. And you will know when you have become the center of the cyclone. There is no need to ask, "How will we know?" How do you know when you have a headache? You simply know.

One of my teachers in school was a very strange man. The first day in his class he said to us, "Remember one thing: headache I don't believe; stomachache I don't believe. I believe only things which I can see. So if you want freedom from school any day, don't make the excuse of a headache, a stomachache, et cetera; you have to bring something real to show me."

And he was thought to be a very strict man. It was very difficult to get even one hour's leave. Just in front of his house there were two *kadamba* trees—very beautiful trees. In the evening he used to go for a walk and it would be almost dark when he returned.

So the first day I said, "It has to be settled." I climbed one of the trees and when he came underneath the tree, I dropped a stone on his head. He screamed, shouted. I came down. I said, "What is the matter?"

He said, "It hurts, and you are asking what is the matter?"

I said, "You have to show it. Unless you show it to me I am not going to believe it. I am your student! And never mention this to anybody—I don't want you tomorrow to call me to the principal's office, because you will be in trouble. You will have to show your hurt, you will have to put it on the table, otherwise it is just fiction; you have invented it; it is imagination. Why should I climb the tree in front of your house? I have never done that in my whole life. Suddenly have I gone mad?"

He said, "Listen, I understand what you want me to understand, but don't tell anybody. If you have a headache I will accept it, but don't tell anybody, because that is my lifelong principle. I am making an exception."

I said, "That's okay. I don't bother about anybody else. Just understand that when I raise my hand, either it is a headache, or it is a stomachache—something invisible. You have to let me go."

The whole class was surprised: "What is the matter? The moment you move your hand, he simply says, 'Get out! Get out immediately!' And the whole day you are free from his torture. But what is the significance of that hand movement? What does it mean? And why does he get so affected?"

You will know; it is far deeper than a headache, and far deeper than a stomachache, far deeper than heartache. It is soul-ache; you will know it.

PRESCRIPTIONS

⟶ DOWN TO EARTH

It is one of the most prevalent problems for the modern man—
the whole of humanity is suffering from uprootedness. When
you become aware of it, you will feel a wavering in the legs,
uncertainty, because the legs are really the roots of man.
Through the legs man is rooted in the earth.

Do two or three things . . .

One: Every morning, if you are near the sea, go to the
beach and run on the sand. If you are not near the sea, then run
anywhere barefoot, with no shoes on, just run on the naked
earth and let there be a contact between the feet and the earth.
Soon, within a few weeks, you will start feeling a great energy
and strength in the legs. So running and barefoot—that's the
first thing.

The second thing is, before you start running and after you
have run, starting and ending, do this: stand with your feet six
or eight inches apart, and close your eyes. Then put your whole
weight first on the right foot, as if you are standing only on the
right. The left is unburdened. Feel it and then shift to the left
foot. Have the whole burden on the left and relieve the right
completely, as if it has nothing to do. It is just there on the earth
but has no weight on it.

Do this four or five times—feeling this shift of energy—and
feel how it feels. Then try to be just in the middle, neither on the
left nor the right, or on both. Just in the middle, no emphasis, fifty-
fifty. That fifty-fifty feeling will give you more rootedness in the
earth. Start and end running with this and it will help very much.

The third thing is to start taking deeper breaths. With shallow breathing one feels uprooted. The breath must go to the very root of your being, and the root is your sex center. Man is born out of sex. The energy is sexual. Breathing should go and make contact with your sex energy so there is a continuous massage of the sex center by the breathing. Then you feel rooted. If your breathing is shallow and it never goes to the sex center, then there is a gap. That gap will give you a wavering, uncertainty, and confusion—a not knowing who you are, not knowing where you are going, not knowing what your purpose is or why you exist; you will feel you are just drifting. Then you will by and by become lusterless, with no life—because how can life be when there is no purpose? And how can there be a purpose when you are not rooted in your own energy?

So first, grounding in the earth—which is the mother of all. Then grounding in the sex center—which is the father of all. Once you are grounded in the earth and the sex center, you will be completely at ease, tranquil, collected, centered, and grounded.

⟶ BREATHE FROM THE SOLES OF THE FEET

The lower part of the body is one of the problems with many people, almost the majority. The lower part has gone dead because sex has been repressed through the centuries. People have become afraid to move below the sex center. They just remain uptight, above the sex center. In fact many people live in their heads, or if they are a little more courageous, they live in the torso.

At the most, people go down to the navel but not beyond that, so half of the body is almost paralyzed, and because of it half of their life is also paralyzed. Then many things become impossible, because the lower part of the body is like roots. These are the roots. The legs are the roots and they connect you with the earth. So people are hanging like ghosts, unconnected with the earth. One has to move back to the feet.

Lao-tzu used to say to his disciples, "Unless you start breathing from the soles of your feet, you are not my disciples. Breathe from the soles of your feet." And he is perfectly right. The deeper you go, the deeper goes your breath. It is almost true to say that the boundary of your being is the boundary of your breath. When the boundary increases and touches your feet, when your breath reaches almost to the feet—not in a physiological sense but in a very deep psychological sense— then you have claimed your whole body. For the first time you are whole, one piece, together.

Go on feeling more and more in the feet.

Sometimes just stand on the earth without shoes and feel the coolness, the softness, and the warmth. Whatever the earth is ready to give in that moment, just feel it and let it flow through you. Allow your energy to flow into the earth and be connected to the earth.

If you are connected to the earth, you are connected to life. If you are connected to the earth, you are connected to your body. If you are connected to the earth, you will become very sensitive and centered—and that's what is needed.

⟶ HARA AWARENESS

Whenever you have nothing to do, just sit silently and move inside and fall into the belly—the center known as the *hara*, just two inches below the navel—and remain there. That will create a great centering of your life energies. You just have to look into it and it will start functioning; you will start feeling that the whole life moves around that center.

It is from the *hara* that life begins and it is in the *hara* that life ends. All our body centers are far away; the *hara* is exactly in the center. That is where we are balanced and rooted. So once one becomes aware of the *hara* many things start happening.

For example, the more you remember the *hara,* the less thinking there will be. Automatically, thinking will become less and less because energy will not move to the head, it will go to the *hara*. The more you think of the *hara,* the more you concentrate there, the more you will find a discipline arising in you. It comes naturally; it is not to be forced. The more aware you are of the *hara* center, the less you will become afraid of life and death, because that is the center of life and death.

Once you become attuned to the *hara* center, you can live courageously. Courage arises out of it—less thinking, more silence, less uncontrolled moments, natural discipline, courage, a rootedness and groundedness.

NIGHT HARBOR

If you feel a sort of wavering left and right and you don't know where your center is, that simply shows that you are no longer in contact with your *hara,* so you have to create that contact.

In the night when you go to sleep, lie down on the bed and put both your hands two inches below the navel, and press a little. Then start breathing, deep breathing, and you will feel that center coming up and going down with the breathing. Feel your whole energy there as if you are shrinking and shrinking and shrinking and you are just existing there as a small center, a very concentrated energy. Just do this for ten or fifteen minutes and then fall asleep.

You can fall asleep doing it; that will be helpful. Then the whole night, that centering persists. Again and again the unconscious goes and centers there. So the whole night without your knowing, you will be coming in many ways in deep contact with the center.

In the morning, the moment that you feel that sleep has gone, don't open the eyes first. Again put your hands there, push a little, and start breathing; again feel the *hara*. Do this for ten or fifteen minutes and then get up. Do this every night and every morning. Within three months you will start feeling centered.

———

It is very essential to have a centering; otherwise one feels fragmentary. Then one is not together, one is just like a jigsaw—all fragments and not a gestalt, not a whole. It is being in bad shape because without a center a man can drag but cannot love. Without a center you can go on doing routine things in your life, but you can never be creative. You will live at the minimum; the maximum will not be possible for you. Only by centering does one live at the maximum, at the zenith, at the peak, at the climax—and that is the only living, a real life.

PROTECTIVE AURA

Every night before you go to sleep, sit in the bed and imagine an aura around your body, just six inches away from your body, the same shape as the body, surrounding you and protecting you. It will become a shield. Do it for four or five minutes and then, still feeling it, go to sleep. Fall into sleep imagining that aura like a blanket around you protecting you so that no tension can enter from the outside, no thought can enter from the outside, and no outside vibrations can enter you. Just feeling that aura, fall asleep.

This has to be done the last thing at night. After it, simply go to sleep so the feeling continues in your unconscious. That is the whole thing. The whole mechanism is that you start by consciously imagining, then you start falling asleep. By and by, when you are on the threshold of sleep, a little imagination continues to linger on. You fall asleep but that little imagination enters the unconscious. That becomes a tremendous force and energy.

We don't know how to protect ourselves from others. Others are not only there, they are broadcasting their being continuously in subtle vibrations. If a tense person passes by, he is simply throwing arrows of tension all around, not particularly addressed to you; he is simply throwing them. He is unconscious; he is not doing it to anybody knowingly. He has to throw off his tension because he is too burdened. He will go mad if he doesn't. It is not that he has *decided* to throw it off; it is overflowing. It is too much and he cannot contain it, so it goes on overflowing.

Somebody passes by and he goes on throwing something at you. If you are receptive and you don't have a protective aura . . . and meditation makes one receptive, very receptive. So when you are alone it is good. When you are surrounded by meditative people, very good. But when you are in the world, in the marketplace, and people are not meditative but are very tense and anxious and have a thousand and one things on their mind, then you just start getting them. You are vulnerable; meditation makes one very soft, so whatsoever comes, enters.

After meditation one has to create a protective aura. Sometimes it happens automatically; sometimes it doesn't. If it is not happening automatically to you, you have to work for it. It will be coming within three months. Anytime between three weeks and three months you will start feeling very, very powerful. So in the night, fall asleep thinking this way.

In the morning the first thought has to be this again. The moment you remember that now sleep is gone, don't open your eyes. Just feel your aura all over the body protecting you. Do it for four or five minutes again and then get up. When you are taking your bath and your tea, go on remembering it. Then in the daytime whenever you feel you have time—sitting in a car or a train or in the office doing nothing—just again relax into it. For a single moment feel it again.

Between three weeks and three months you will start feeling it almost like a solid thing. It will surround you and you will be able to feel that you can now pass amidst a crowd and you will remain unaffected, untouched. It will make you tremendously happy because now only your problems will be your problems, nobody else's.

It is very easy to solve one's own problems because they are one's own. It is very difficult when you go on getting others' problems; then you cannot solve them because in the first place they don't belong to you.

Try to create a protective aura and you will be able to see it and its function. You will see that you are completely protected. Wherever you go, things will be coming to you but they will be returned; they will not touch you.

⚊ BALANCING ACT

The right and left sides of your brain function separately; everybody's does this, but when meditation hits you deeply, the separation and the difference can become exaggerated.

Sit silently by yourself and press your eyes. Press the eyeballs until you start seeing lights. Don't hurt the eyes too much, but a little hurt is allowed. Just go on watching those lights. That will settle many things.

Do this for four or five minutes—pressing the eyes—and then relax for five minutes, then press them again. Do this for forty minutes and then just splash cool water over them. Close your eyes and feel the coolness.

Do this for fifteen days. This exercise will settle many things in the brain and you will feel very collected and sane.

BEING HERE

As you grow in consciousness, the world itself starts changing. Nothing needs to be done directly; all the changes happen almost of their own accord. The only thing that is needed is an effort to be more conscious.

Start becoming more and more conscious of everything that you are doing. Walking, walk consciously; bring your total attention to walking. There is a great difference between when you just walk without any consciousness and when you bring the quality of consciousness to walking. The change is radical. It may not be visible from the outside, but from the inside it is really moving into another dimension.

Try some small act: for example, moving your hand, you can move it mechanically. Then move it with great consciousness, slowly, slowly, feeling the movement and looking from inside at how you are moving it.

Just in this small gesture you are on the threshold of the divine, because a miracle is happening. It is one of the greatest mysteries that science has not yet been able to fathom. You decide that you should move the hand and the hand follows your decision. It is a miracle because it is consciousness contacting matter . . . not only that, matter is following consciousness. The bridge has not yet been found. It is magic. It is the power of the mind over matter; that's what magic is all about. You do it the whole day, but you have not done it consciously; otherwise in this simple gesture a great meditation will arise in you. This is the way the divine is moving the whole existence.

So walking, sitting, listening, or talking, remain alert.

⟿ COLLECTING YOURSELF

With each breath going out, say "one." As the breath goes out, say "one"; breathe in and don't say anything. Breathe out and say "one"; breathe in and don't say anything. So with each outgoing breath you simply say "One . . . one . . . one." Not only say it but also feel that the whole existence is one, it is a unity. Don't repeat that, just have that feeling—and saying "one" will help.

Do this for twenty minutes every day and make it a point that nobody disturbs you while you are doing it. You can open your eyes and look at the clock, but don't set the alarm. Anything that can give you a jerk will be bad, so don't keep the phone in the room where you are doing it, and nobody should knock. For those twenty minutes you have to be absolutely relaxed. If there is too much noise around, use earplugs.

Saying "one" with each exhalation will make you so calm and quiet and collected, you cannot imagine. Do this in the daytime, never at night; otherwise your sleep will be disturbed because this will be so relaxing that you will not feel sleepy. You will feel fresh. The best time is the morning, otherwise the afternoon, but never at night.

⌁ Lao-tzu's Secret

I will now tell you of a secret sutra from Lao-tzu. It is not written anywhere but has been handed down by word of mouth to his disciples through the ages. It is a sutra on a method of meditation.

Lao-tzu says: Sit cross-legged. Feel that there is a weighing scale within you. Each side of the scale is near each breast. The pointer is between your eyes, where the third eye is supposed to be. The strings of the scale are in your brain. Be conscious of this scale within you for all twenty-four hours of the day and be mindful that the pans on both sides are at the same level, and the pointer is straight in the middle. If you can balance these scales within, you have completed your journey.

But it is very difficult. You will find that with a slight breath, the sides of the scale go up and down. You are sitting quietly—suddenly a person enters the room and the weighing scales move up and down. Lao-tzu says, "Balance your consciousness. The opposites should be equalized and the middle hand should remain fixed in the center. Whether life brings happiness or unhappiness, light or darkness, honor or dishonor, keep your eye on the balance within and keep adjusting it."

One day it will reach the perfect balance—where there is not life but existence, where there are no waves but the ocean; where there is no "I" but all.

➤ Visualize the Buddha Within

At least once a day you have to find time; any time will do, whenever you can find time, but it is good to do it when the stomach is empty. More energy is available when the stomach is empty. Not that one should be hungry—just that the stomach should not be too full. If you have eaten, then after two or three hours. Just a cup of tea is good; a cup of tea is very helpful.

The second thing: If you can take a bath before it, that will be very helpful. Take a hot bath and a cold shower. First soak yourself in a hot bath and then just take a cold, two-minute shower. End with a cold shower; that will prepare you perfectly.

Then take a cup of tea and sit; make yourself comfortable. If you can sit on the floor, you can have a pillow underneath; that will be good. If it feels difficult or the posture is difficult, you can sit on a chair.

Relax the whole body and just concentrate on the middle of your chest, just in the middle where the rib bones end and the stomach starts. With closed eyes, imagine that a small Buddha statue is there, just an outline of a Buddha statue. You can have a picture of a small Buddha statue so that you can figure it out. Just a two-inch-high Buddha statue.

Visualize that it is made of light and that rays are spreading out from it. Get absorbed in it so you can go into it easily . . . rays spreading, filling your whole body.

If you can sit in a Buddha posture on the floor, that will be very helpful because that figure and your posture will fit together. The rays are spreading and the whole body becomes full of light. Then the rays start spreading outside the body— just a visualization inside. The rays start touching the ceiling and the walls and soon they are going outside the room; they go on spreading and they go on spreading. Within fifteen minutes' time let them cover the whole universe, as far as you can conceive.

Great peace will arise. Remain in that state for ten minutes—the whole universe full of rays, and the center of that in your innermost heart. Hold that state for ten minutes. Go on contemplating it; go on feeling the rays; go on and on and on. The whole universe is full of those rays.

Then start shrinking back, slowly—as slowly as you had gone out, slowly shrink back. Then come back to your inner Buddha—again the two-inch-high statue full of light.

Then suddenly let it disappear abruptly. That is the point, the most significant point in the whole process. Let is disappear abruptly and a negative image will be left. It is just like when you look into a window too long and then you close your eyes and you see the negative image of the window. The Buddha statue has been there, full of light; suddenly, abruptly, let it disappear. There will be a dark Buddha statue, a negative statue, emptiness. Hold that for five to ten minutes—that hole, that emptiness.

In the first stage, when the rays are spreading all over the universe, you will feel great peace such as you might never have felt before, and a great expansion, a feeling that you have become huge and that the whole universe is in you.

In the second stage, instead of peace you will feel blissfulness. When the Buddha statue becomes negative and all light disappears and there is darkness and silence, you will feel a great blissfulness for no reason at all! A well-being is arising in you—hold that.

So this whole process has to take not more than forty-five minutes, forty-five to sixty minutes.

This can be done in bed at night when you are going to sleep; that is the most perfect time. Do it and then just fall into sleep so the same state will continue vibrating the whole night. Many times in your dreams that Buddha statue will appear; many times in your dreams those rays will be felt. In the morning you will feel that your sleep has been of a totally different quality. It was not just sleep: something more positive than sleep has been there; some presence has been there. You will come out more rejuvenated, more alert, and more full of reverence for life.

✐ FIND THE INNER ZERO

Before you go to sleep, do this. Just lying down on the bed with closed eyes, imagine a blackboard, as black as you can imagine. Then visualize on the blackboard the figure three, three times. First visualize it and wipe it out; again visualize it and wipe it out; again visualize it and wipe it out. Then visualize the figure two, three times; then visualize the figure one, three times; then visualize the figure zero, three times. By the time you reach the third zero, you will feel a great silence unlike you have ever felt before.

Someday you will fall into absolute silence, as if the whole existence has suddenly disappeared and nothing is. That will be a great glimpse.

So in the night while you are going sleep, do this simple process—just lying down on the bed—but remember to complete it because that process gives so much silence. It is a simple process and will not take more than two or three minutes at the most, but you might fall asleep before you have completed it. Try to complete it, don't go to sleep—the third zero has to come—and don't go in a hurry, go slowly and lovingly.

ABOUT THE AUTHOR

Osho's teachings defy categorization, covering everything from the individual quest for meaning to the most urgent social and political issues facing society today. His books are not written but are transcribed from audio and video recordings of extemporaneous talks given to international audiences over a period of thirty-five years. Osho has been described by *The Sunday Times* (London) as one of the "1,000 Makers of the Twentieth Century" and by American author Tom Robbins as "the most dangerous man since Jesus Christ."

About his own work Osho has said that he is helping to create the conditions for the birth of a new kind of human being. He has often characterized this new human being as "Zorba the Buddha"—capable of enjoying both the earthy pleasures of a Zorba the Greek and the silent serenity of a Gautama Buddha. Running like a thread through all aspects of Osho's work is a vision that encompasses both the timeless wisdom of the East and the highest potential of Western science and technology.

Osho is also known for his revolutionary contribution to the science of inner transformation, with an approach to meditation that acknowledges the accelerated pace of contemporary life. His unique Active Meditations are designed to first release the accumulated stresses of body and mind, so that it is easier to experience the thought-free and relaxed state of meditation.

OSHO MEDITATION RESORT®

The Osho Meditation Resort is a place where people can have a direct personal experience of a new way of living with more alertness, relaxation, and fun. Located about a hundred miles southeast of Mumbai in Pune, India, the resort offers a variety of programs to thousands of people who visit each year from more than a hundred countries around the world.

Originally developed as a summer retreat for maharajas and wealthy British colonialists, Pune is now a thriving modern city that is home to a number of universities and high-tech industries. The Meditation Resort spreads over forty acres in a tree-lined suburb known as Koregaon Park. The resort campus provides accommodation for a limited number of guests, and there is a plentiful variety of nearby hotels and private apartments available for stays of a few days up to several months.

Resort programs are all based in the Osho vision of a qualitatively new kind of human being who is able to both participate creatively in everyday life and relax into silence and meditation. Most programs take place in modern, air-conditioned facilities and include a variety of individual sessions, courses, and workshops covering everything from creative arts to holistic health treatments, personal transformation and therapy, esoteric sciences, the Zen approach to sports and recreation, relationship issues, and significant life transitions for men and women. Individual sessions and group workshops are offered throughout the year, alongside a full daily schedule of meditations.

Outdoor cafés and restaurants within the resort grounds serve both traditional Indian fare and a choice of international dishes, all made with organically grown vegetables from the commune's own farm. The campus has its own private supply of safe, filtered water.

See www.osho.com/resort for more information, including travel tips, course schedules, and guesthouse bookings.

For more information about Osho and his work, see www.osho.com, a comprehensive website in several languages that includes an online tour of the Meditation Resort and a calendar of its course offerings, a catalog of books and tapes, a list of Osho information centers worldwide, and selections from Osho's talks.

You may also contact Osho International New York, oshointernational@oshointernational.com.

OSHO®
SOMETHING FOR EVERYONE

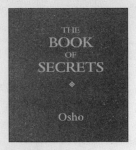

THE BOOK OF SECRETS

Contemporary instructions and guidance for 112 meditation techniques, based on original sacred teachings from India. A unique and insightful overview of the entire science of meditation which allows individuals to find the method that suits them best.

ISBN: 0-312-18058-6 Hardcover $35.00/$46.99 Can.

THE BOOK OF SECRETS:
KEYS TO LOVE AND MEDITATION

The audio companion to *The Book of Secrets*.

ISBN: 1-55927-486-7 Audio Cassette $16.95/$23.50 Can.

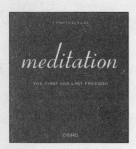

MEDITATION: THE FIRST AND LAST FREEDOM

A practical guide to integrating meditation into all aspects of daily life, which includes instructions for over 60 meditation techniques, including the revolutionary Osho Active Meditations™.

ISBN: 0-312-16927-2 Paperback $13.95/$17.99 Can.
ISBN: 0-312-14820-8 Hardcover $22.95/$35.99 Can.

 **TAKE A NEW LOOK** www.OSHO.com

Osho is a registered trademark of Osho International Foundation.